AF292110

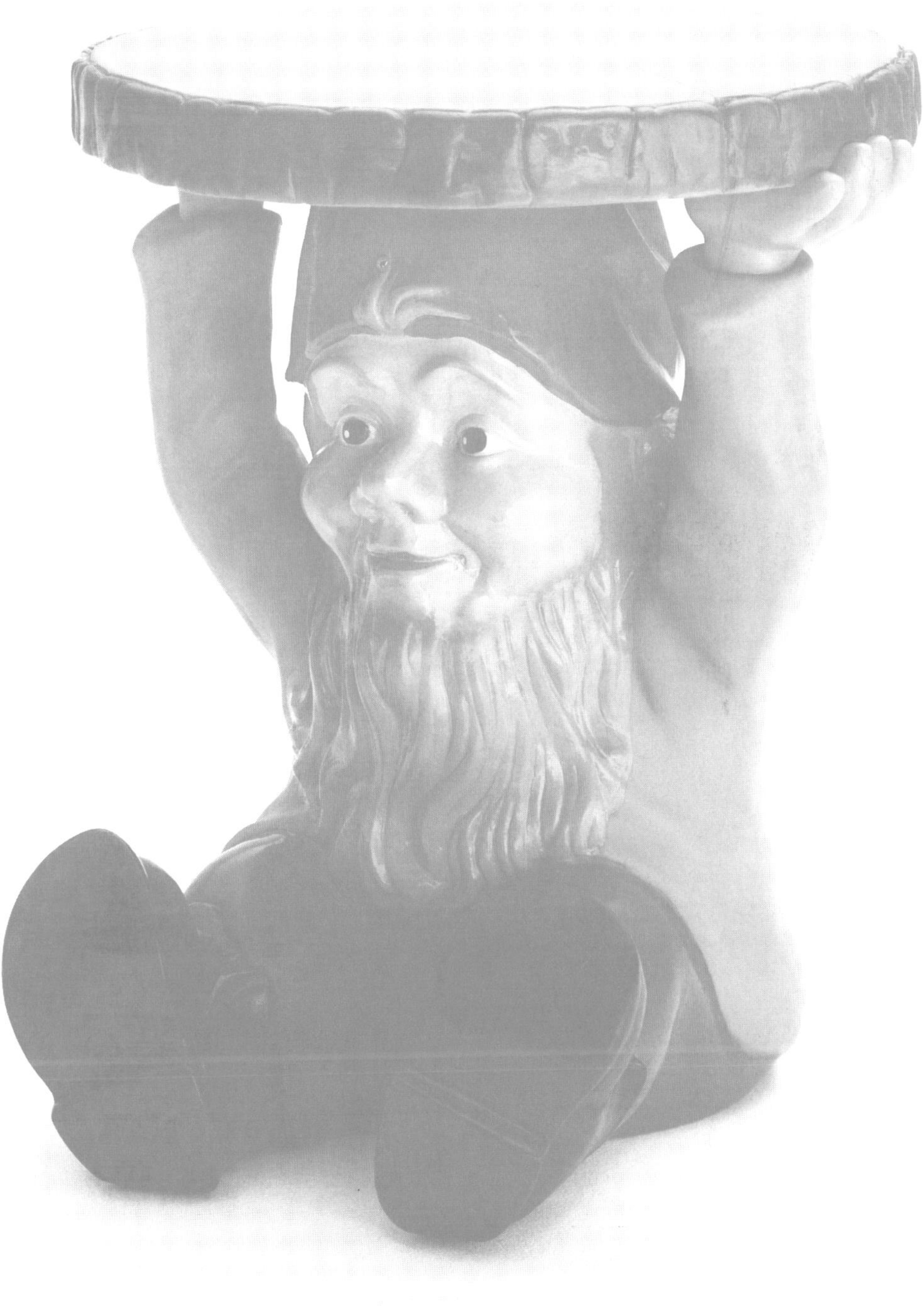

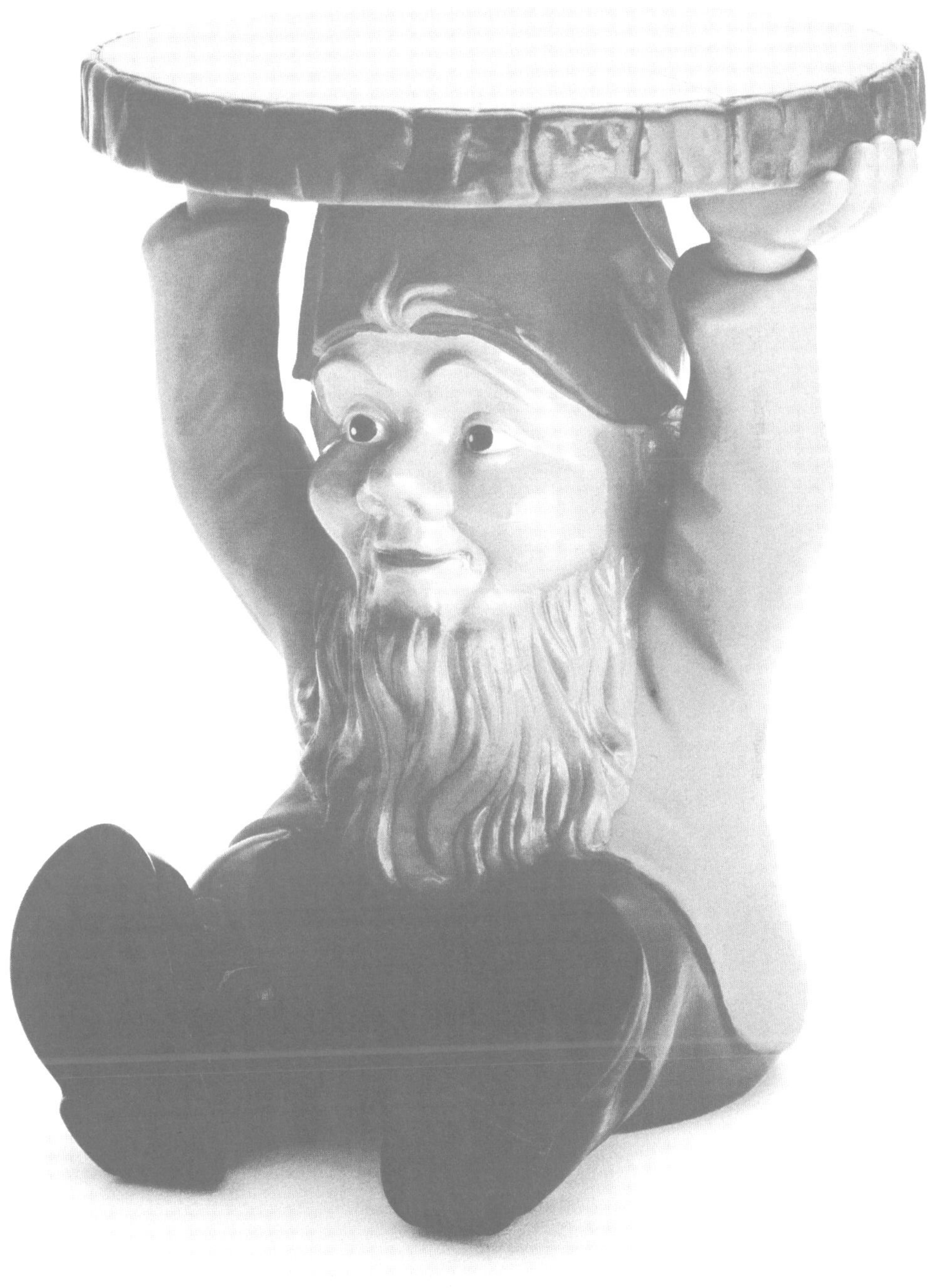

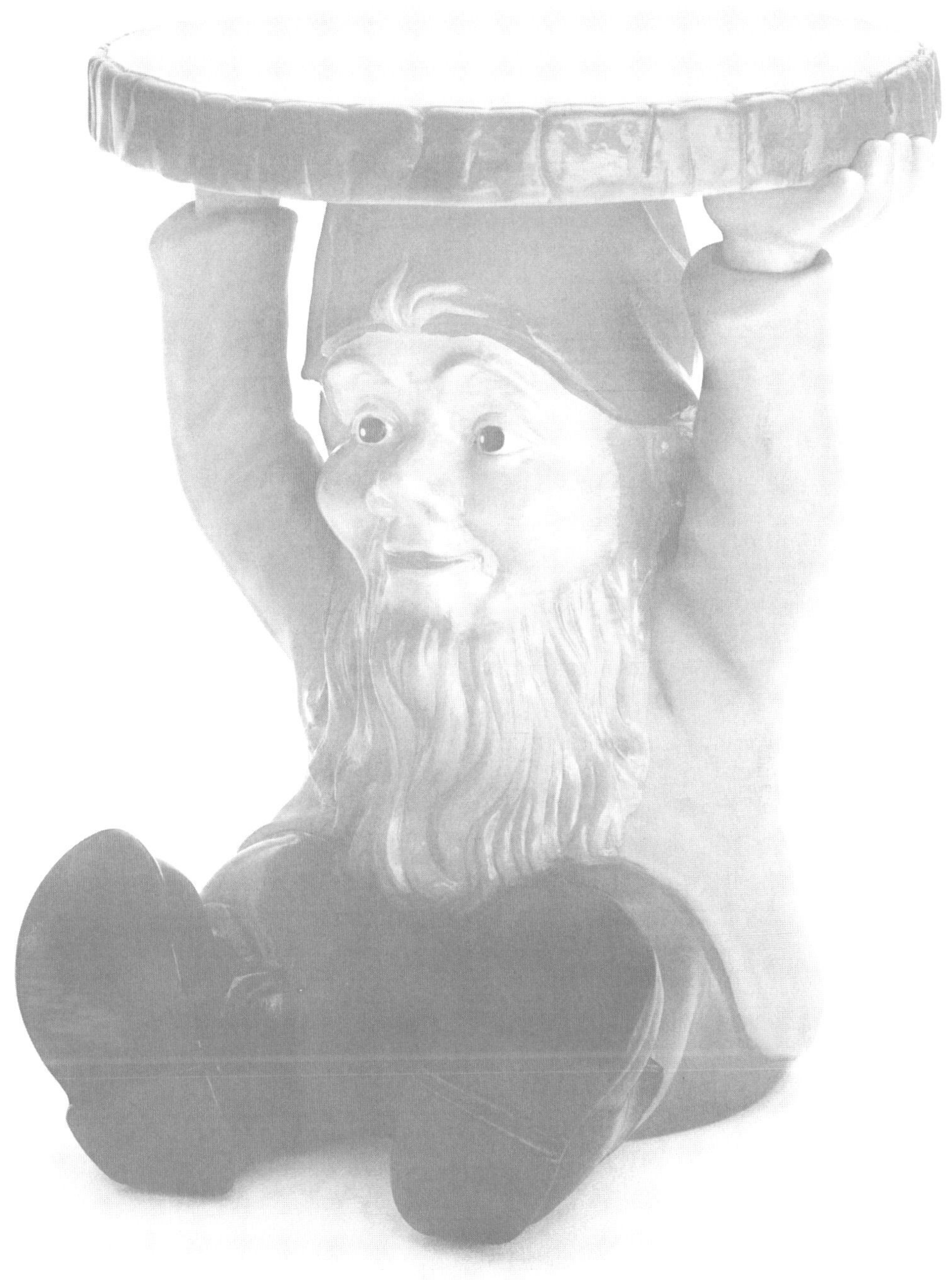

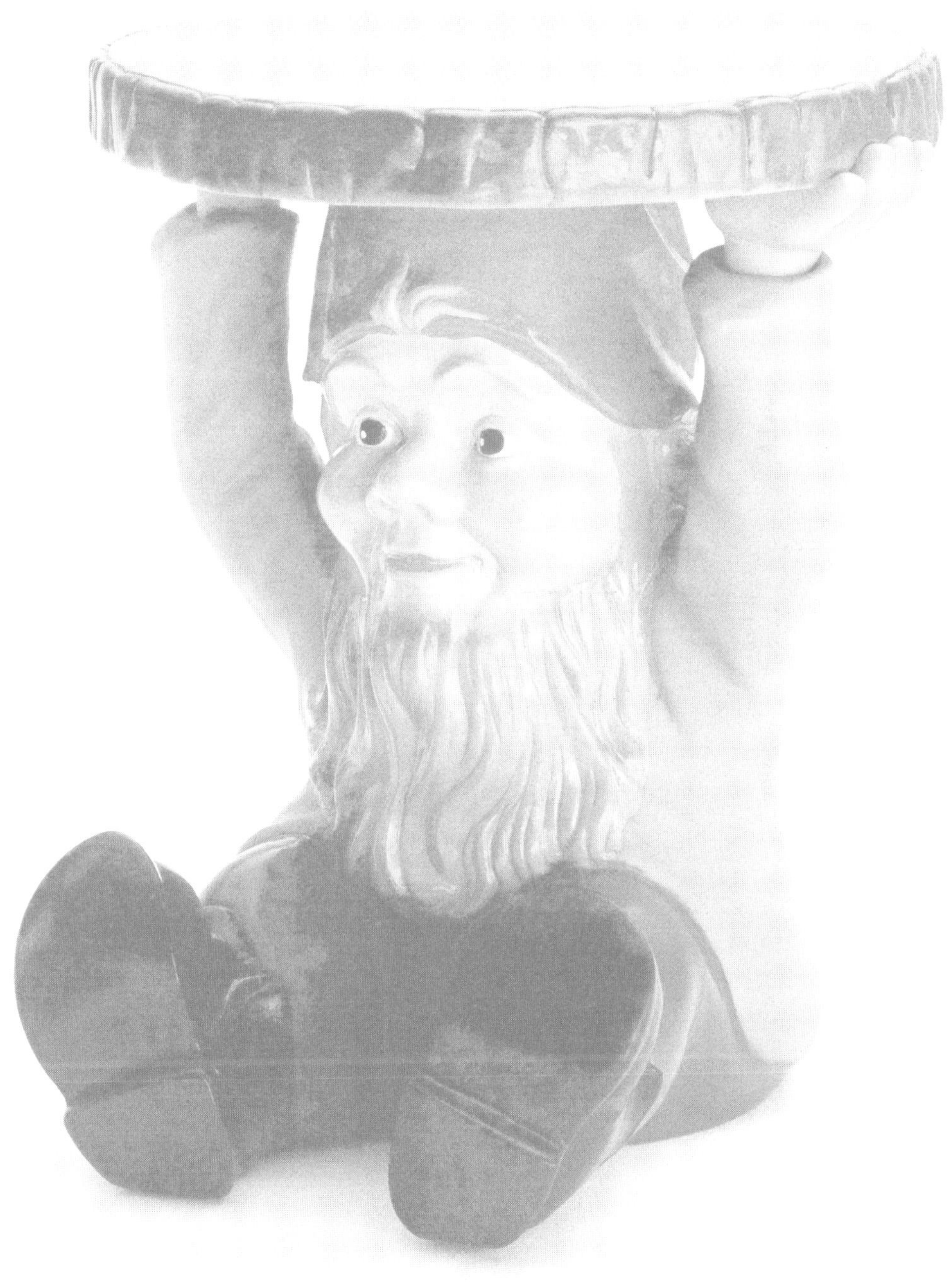

SIMON

MARTIN

27 **Foreword**
Elena Hill

29 **Introduction**
Steven Bode

31 **You Are**
Dan Fox

37 **Feeling**
Melissa Gronlund

43 **The Milky Way**
Neil Mulholland

49 Carlton

65 Louis Ghost Chair

83 UR Feeling

101 **Biography**
102 **List of works**

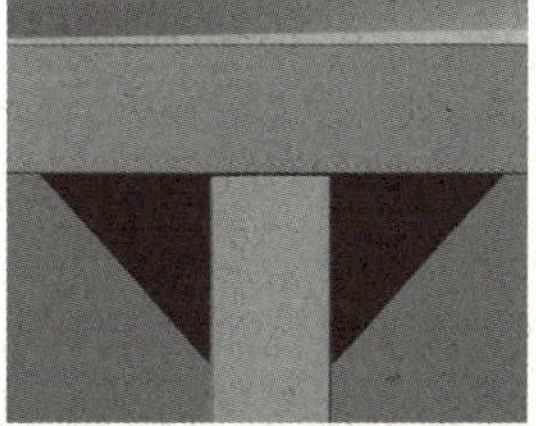

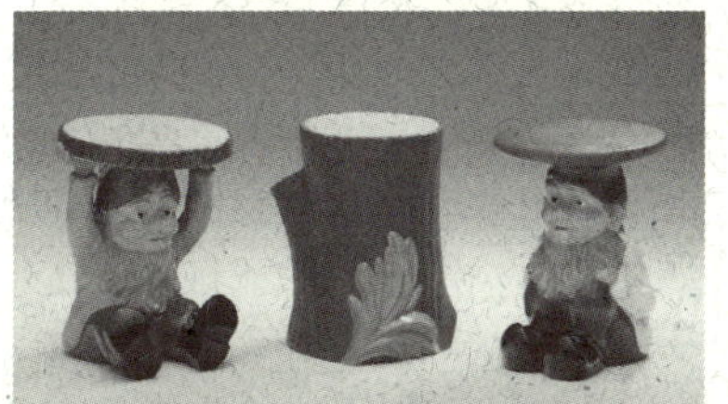

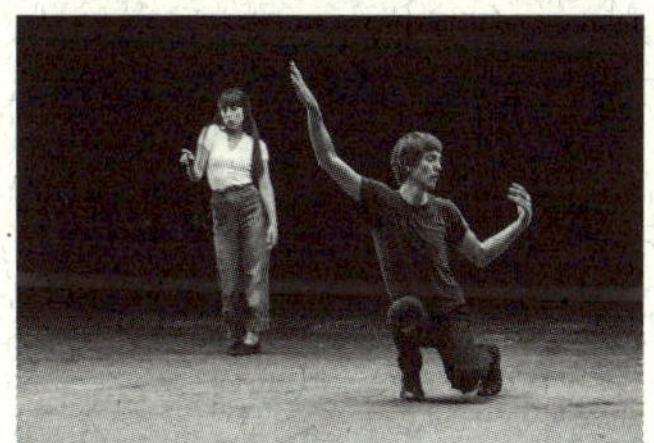

This publication was born out of a single film commission, *Louis Ghost Chair.* Dr. Alexander (Xa) Sturgis, at the time, Director of the Holburne Museum in Bath, approached me to help the museum embark upon a contemporary moving image project. It would be the museum's first film commission. With this in mind, I knew that Steven Bode and his team at Film and Video Umbrella (FVU) would be an assured and considerate third partner.

Xa, Steven and I met over the course of a few weeks looking through several artists' work in order to all agree on an artist that would best suit what is at the heart of the Holburne Museum – the personal collection of Sir William Holburne (1793–1874), his life-long interest in art and his enthusiasm for collecting.

Through generous support of Arts Council England and FVU's commitment to expanding the reach of artists' moving-image we were able to resource a publication, which would round out the context of Simon's work to eventually include *Carlton*, *Louis Ghost Chair* and *UR Feeling.*

I would like to thank all three writers, Dan Fox, Melissa Gronlund and Neil Mulholland, for seamlessly weaving together all three pieces. I would also like to say thank you to all the individuals, institutions, colleagues and friends who have supported this publication and the works' production. Everyone came together through a wonderful sense of cooperative purpose and generosity.

Simon Martin's film *Louis Ghost Chair* (2012) occupies a pivotal place in his
artistic practice. Audaciously conceived, deftly materialised and impeccably
crafted, this short visual essay (on the theme of a classic armchair and its
contemporary appropriation and reproduction) encapsulates exactly what
it is about Martin's work that makes it so distinctive and appealing. One
of a growing number of films and videos that Martin has made over the last
decade, *Louis Ghost Chair* also occupies a central place in a loose trilogy
of pieces that, in honour of its subject, we might be tempted to describe
as a suite of works. Bookended and completed by *Carlton* (2006), and
UR Feeling (2015), this *ad hoc* three-piece, embodying different styles,
and gathered from disparate sources, nonetheless fits (and sits) together
neatly, revealing both Martin's eye for an individual object, and his ability
to fashion a larger *mise-en-scène*.

It may be that gift for composition that makes one think of a suite in another
sense of the word. Discrete yet harmonious, this trio of films showcases
many of Martin's trademark motifs, repeated and extended in a way that
develops ideas and steadily builds momentum. In this instance, *Carlton*
(an eclectic, speculative rumination on an iconic item of furniture, namely
a bookcase created by the radical Milanese design group, Memphis) acts
as an ideal prelude to *Louis Ghost Chair*, and its more formal reprising
of similar, re-stated themes. Taking us back to the beginning, even as
it completes a cycle, *UR Feeling* shifts tone dramatically. After two films
that revolve around particular items of furniture (and the spirit of the times
that can be elicited from them), this disarming coda has a very different
object in its sights. Indeed, as its title implies, it is maybe not any one
object at all, more a *feeling* of what once existed, but which still casts its
light, or its shadow, over the contemporary scene; an indefinable presence,
reverberating in the built environment around us, that continues to affect
us, inform us, even shape us.

If Martin's favourite key is minor (subtle, understated), his subject matter
is contrastingly major (art historical, philosophical, phenomenological,

polemical). His films are deceptive: they insinuate themselves slowly but, in their meticulous, careful iteration, generate their own affective presence; one that resonates and percolates in the mind. For this publication, we asked three writers to reflect on the trio of *Carlton*, *Louis Ghost Chair* and *UR Feeling* and their significance within Martin's aesthetic as a whole. Dan Fox, Melissa Gronlund and Neil Mulholland have responded brilliantly to that brief, producing texts that are creative, associative, anecdotal, experimental, insightful and inventive. Taken together, these three essays provide an eloquent summary of Simon Martin's preoccupations and concerns. In their different ways, they also help to illuminate a practice whose pleasures are often in the details but which, in the agility of its approach and the breadth of its imagination, adds up to much, much more than the sum of its parts.

I am eight years old, and standing in the living room at home. I am clutching a red 'Darth Vader' plastic lunchbox and wearing my black parka, ready to go to school. It's the middle of winter: one of those bitter, wet, February mornings trying to drag itself into grey-white, half-hearted daylight. The furry hood of my coat is up and Mum is putting her coat on, about to take me to school. I am feeling anxious, melancholy in ways that I am too young to understand. In front of me is a wobbly wooden chair, with a wide circular back supported by carved spindles. It's old – farm furniture from my grandparents. The wood is black from use. And here's the thing: I clearly remember thinking, at that moment, how lucky the chairs are, and wishing I could be one of them. Life as a chair would be so much simpler. I wouldn't have to go out into the cold. I could stay at home and never go to school again, never face the complications, disappointments and confusions of childhood. I would willingly give up running around, playing with toys and all the other things that boys my age do, and abdicate all responsibility in order to inhabit the form and consciousness of a chair.

Before Mum hustles me out into the rain, I put my face flat against the chair and examine the grain of the wood. I imagine the lines and striations to be rivers and canyons, the knots to be lakes or whirlpools. I examine small holes left by woodworm, and globs of glue at the ends of the spindles where Dad has tried to fix the backrest. I long to dive deeper into the chair, become a human microscope exploring at molecular level, or shrink myself like the intrepid scientists swimming through the human body in *Fantastic Voyage*. At atomic eye-level, wood looks like a honeycomb of caves and craters – it resembles the moon, or the interior of a beehive. Wood, at x300 magnification, does not appear to be wood. You could say it has a concealed identity, in the way that many materials do. Take plastic, for instance. Walk plastic a step back from its form as a school lunchbox or nylon black parka, and you arrive at a liquid product of the petrochemical industry, which if you move back further is oil, which, leaping even further back, is formed underground over billions of years from dead insects, plants and minerals. But as the narrator of Simon Martin's film *Louis Ghost Chair* tells us – in

a voice with the calm authority of a museum audio guide crossed with
a therapist – 'there is the way of plastic and there is the way of wood.'

As Martin's camera slowly probes the delicately carved legs and arms of
an 18th century Louis XV chair, this voice explains that the way of wood is
to never forget its materiality. A tree is cut and shaped into an elegant piece
of furniture, but unless the material has been painted or laminated, we can
always see that wood is wood. The material carries the inscription of the
gesture of its manufacture; of carving, turning, joinery, sanding, varnishing.
The film then turns its attention to a transparent plastic 'Louis Ghost Chair',
designed in 2000 by Philippe Starck for the company Kartell. It's modelled
after the classic Louis XV seat, a mixture of textbook postmodern nods-and-
winks and 'heritage values'. The narrator observes that we think of plastic
as existing in whatever form it arrives to us as. We do not think of a plastic
chair in the raw, as a toxic liquid polymer waiting for shape. This is the way
of plastic, and the material carries with it the inscription of manufacturing
process; of extrusion, injection moulding, colour dosing, process cooling,
rotational moulding, vacuum forming.

The ways of wood and plastic, however, only partially explain what Martin's
narrator calls 'the pull of physical things'. (A phrase that could arguably
be taken as the regimental motto for all Martin's work.) *Louis Ghost Chair*
asks us to think about the long journey of a chair from an 18th century
workshop in France to its existence today; sat in the corner of a National
Trust stately home, say, or being auctioned at Christie's where it might
find a new home in Moscow, Dubai or Beijing. The film asks: 'what keeps
the chair holding steady?' What qualities allow us to recognise a shape
carved in Paris over 200 years ago in a plastic mass-produced chair
decorating the lobby of a boutique hotel in New York?

Were we to travel back in time and find ourselves on a wet weekday
morning in that Paris atelier – perhaps a few years before revolution
gives the artisan a new perspective on his place in the social order – we
might see that chair and declare: 'This is tomorrow.' Or ask: 'Just what is
it that makes today's homes so different, so appealing?' Making art in the
present is always about packing for the future. In Martin's film *Carlton*, the
same museum-guide-therapist that guides us through *Louis Ghost Chair*
reassures us that 'Nobody knows exactly when "today" actually happened.
Maybe "today" occurred with the closure of Andy Warhol's Factory, or with
the growth in the secondary market for avant-garde furniture [...] Perhaps
it is the point when one notices elderly people eating in McDonald's for the
first time or realise that you know the lyrics to "West End Girls" by the Pet
Shop Boys by heart.' Today is the moment you register change, recalibrate
your relationship to the world according to your age and experiences; it's
when you understand that the clothes you wear, the car you drive, and the

music you listen to now broadcasts on a different frequency to the one you first tuned into. In this sense, *Carlton* is about something 'more emotional than functional'.

'How do you make a film about a piece of furniture?' the narrator asks. The question is rhetorical, Martin's courtesy to the structuralists and Brechtians watching from the peanut gallery. *Carlton* is about so much more than a piece of furniture. The film begins as an essay on the Memphis group's colourful and totemic 'Carlton' shelving unit, produced in 1981 using a playful combination of materials: Formica, imitation wood, marble. From here Martin argues that the equivocal attitude towards materials set by Memphis has spread into the world like a 'mutated postmodern gene', today seen in the 'chrome, plastic wood, real wood, Perspex and cast-concrete flagstones' that can be found everywhere 'from a cocktail bar in Liverpool [...] to a car showroom in Cape Town.'

In 'Post Modern', an essay for *Harpers & Queen* published a year before Memphis produced 'Carlton', Peter York describes London in 1980 as a place where 'the time frames are utterly scrambled, the past is all around: in that world the notions of either rejecting or embracing the past look irrelevant. Postmodernism, which deals with the past like one huge antique supermarket, looks very relevant indeed. Pastiche and parody is just an uncomfortable transition to a time when period references will be used without any self-consciousness.' The age of the antique-modern supermarket sweep arrived with us some years ago. Look around you. Examine what the *Carlton* narrator nails as 'a generalised environment of quote, reference and approximation, a place of perpetual refurbishment and all-purpose vernacular.' The sociologist Sharon Zukin, in her book *Naked City: The Death and Life of Authentic Urban Places*, observes in cities such as London and New York 'a trend toward an aesthetic rather than a political view of social life.' Full sleeve tattoos and a Black Flag t-shirt no longer, as they once did, mark you out as a person deeply committed to alternative lifestyles. Knowing the difference between soba and ramen noodles does not mean you're an adventurous traveller, conversant in the culture and cuisine of East Asia. In New York you can buy twenty-dollar lobster rolls from food trucks on the street, and hear The Stone Roses used as muzak in the cash machine lobbies of Chase Manhattan bank. Fancy a drink? Let's go to that bar that serves small-batch bourbon in jam-jars and where the staff dress like extras from *Boardwalk Empire*.

As Zukin writes, urban 'authenticity has taken on a different meaning that has little to do with origins and a lot to do with style. The concept has migrated from a quality of people to a quality of things, and most recently to a quality of experiences.' Style has always been a question of survival in cities – a way of navigating other people and carving your own corner – but today the flat field of equivocal reference and quote is harder to work with, perhaps because its ubiquity is tied up in that knot of things 'more emotional than functional.' This ubiquity of reference, one that's both historical and emotional, is what Martin's films attempt to describe. They evoke the end of Whit Stillman's 1998 film *The Last Days of Disco*, when the character Des McGrath says to his friend: 'You know that Shakespearean admonition, "To thine own self be true"? It's premised on the idea that "thine own self" is something pretty good, being true to which is commendable. But what if "thine own self" is not so good? What if it's pretty bad? Would it be better, in that case, not to be true to "thine own self"?' How do you make a film about cultural authenticity? Make a film about a piece of furniture.

But be sure to then cut to a scene featuring what looks very much like Donald Judd's *Untitled* sculpture from 1963: an iron pipe inset into the top of a plywood box covered in light cadmium red oil paint. Martin shifts from chairs to minimalist sculpture in *Louis Ghost Chair*, juxtaposing the 'Judd' with the Louis furniture, along with three Starck-designed table-stools, hand-painted and made from batch-dyed thermoplastic technopolymer in the shape of kitsch garden gnomes. (The gnomes are named Atilla, Napoleon and Saint-Esprit, but what that says about Starck's relationship to power and spirituality is anyone's guess.) The utility value of the chairs and gnomes is contrasted with the 'Judd', assembled from readymade materials only for the occasion of the sculpture. The 'Judd' is an intellectually high-net-worth object; something for the connoisseurs, like the original Louis XV chair. Atilla, Napoleon, Saint-Esprit and the 'Louis Ghost Chair' revel in game play; antique furniture is made into pop, and cheap garden ornaments are elevated to design object. 'Plywood is plywood,' says Martin's narrator. 'Iron pipe is iron pipe. Cadmium red oil paint is cadmium red oil paint. 1963 is 1963. A camera pointed at something is a camera pointed at something.' In this Judd work, you can see the nails that hold the plywood together, the points at which the pieces of wood join to make the box. The paint looks to have been applied by hand. In later years, Judd would have his works made by professional fabricators, erasing the trace of his hand, rationalising the surfaces of his sculptures. But his 'specific objects', rather than becoming more specific, instead accrued historical patina, and like a Louis XV chair started to tell other stories.

In 'Sincerity and Authenticity', a series of lectures given in 1970, the critic Lionel Trilling argued that '[authenticity] is a word of ominous import. As we use it in reference to human existence, its provenance is the museum, where persons expert in such matters test whether objects of art are what they appear to be or are claimed to be, and therefore worth the price that is asked for them – or, if this has already been paid, worth the admiration

they are being given.' What were those lines in *Louis Ghost Chair* again?
'Iron pipe is iron pipe. Cadmium red oil paint is cadmium red oil paint.
1963 is 1963.' Perhaps. Minimalism as a New York art movement only
lasted for a brief period: it wouldn't be long until the minimal aesthetic
was used as a backdrop for selling property and mixing expensive cocktails.
It became the international shorthand for contemporary sophistication.
The 'loft-living' lifestyle pioneered by artists such as Judd in the SoHo
of 1960s New York is today beyond the reach of many creative people,
and the story of SoHo is not dissimilar to the story of Judd rationalising
his sculpture: small-manufacture displaced by 'creative' industry, which
is then booted out by high-end retail and Wall Street traders looking
for a bit of ersatz bohemian rough. Judd's five-storey SoHo loft is now
a museum surrounded by corporate chain stores and luxury boutiques.
The neighbourhood's historic ironwork buildings have been preserved,
but the atmosphere is haunted, like the transparent plastic Starck chair.
How do you make a film about hyper-gentrification and the construction
of 'authenticity' by economics and power? Make a film about a sculpture.

'A camera pointed at something is a camera pointed at something.' In
Louis Ghost Chair Martin shoots his subjects against a perfect white infinity
curve. Seen in isolation from any context, the chairs, gnomes and 'Judd' look
like specimens in a laboratory, although not necessarily a scientific one. It
could be a cosmetics lab — the sort of fictional environment of a television
ad, in which scientists endorse hand-creams and shampoo. The objects
might be the subjects of a fashion shoot, props being readied to leverage
emotion and feeling in order to persuade you to buy something, or simply
readied to enter the image economy as themselves, to be dropped into the
flow of experience. *Carlton*, by contrast, is based on a pre-existing image
from a book. Martin's camera smoothly tracks along coloured shelves
and drawers, but it rarely moves to the side or behind the furniture unit.
If *Carlton* is a film about reproduction and surfaces, and *Louis Ghost
Chair* is a meditation on materials and objecthood, then Martin's latest
film, *UR-Feeling*, is an evocation. Narrative is absent; we simply see
two figures in a room, or rather, a schematic suggestion of a room. Their
gestures are attempts to express mental images, colour the room with
what's inside the head. *UR-Feeling* is a mood — a film about the intangibles
that press in on us. Think of it like music: an invisible force that seizes
control of your body — the bone-shaking bass frequencies of dub, for
example — or like a scent in the air, half-heard ambient music.

How do you write an essay about a film with no words? Try conjuring
an atmosphere. Eight years after that morning when I wished I was a chair,
I began visiting London on my own. As a condition of these day trips to
the big city, Mum and Dad insisted I get back in time for dinner. This meant
I'd take an early morning coach there from my hometown, often arriving

before shops and museums opened. It was during those moments that
I absorbed London's atmospheres: sitting in a café with a cup of coffee
and a book waiting for the Tate to open, or walking down Berwick Street
on a foggy morning in search of a record shop. I found these atmospheres
as intoxicating, if not more so, as any cultural experience the city had
to offer. London became a feeling. Smell the warm air pushed through
a Tube station by an approaching train. Look at the dirty yellow of London
brick. Listen to the throaty grumble of a cab engine and feel the sticky
beer-soaked wooden table in a Sam Smith's pub. Martin's films describe
the way of wood, and the way of plastic. They present us with the way of
the image and the way of the object, and echo-locate the ways of you, me,
London, New York, Sao Paulo, Liverpool and Cape Town. You are feeling
something. Press your face against it and look closely at the grain.

Dan Fox – 'Danny Fox', to Simon Martin – opens his essay in this book
with an anecdote about a wooden chair he once pushed his face against,
to feel the grain, as a boy not wanting to go outside in the cold. He
uses this memory as the foil against which a number of manifestations
of inauthenticity is set – terms and concepts like pastiche, style and
postmodernism – sketching out the two poles which Martin's work
oscillates between. Martin's work has investigated these notions almost
throughout his career, conceived from the very general – even his early
film, *Wednesday Afternoon* (2005), which tracks a walk through a museum,
could be said to approach the question of posture via representation
in general – to more specific and canonical examples of postmodernism,
such as *Memphis* and *Louis Ghost Chair*, both of which Fox's essay
considers in depth.

Lately, however, and largely owing to circumstances beyond Martin's
control, these questions of the authentic and inauthentic have acquired
new parameters, and with them, new urgency. Suddenly one is able to
create documentation of things that aren't real, as Martin did in *Untitled*
(2008), where he used a stock image – in this case, of a tree frog – to
create digitally a video of a reptile that doesn't exist in actual life. The
idea of the 'stock image' as background information becomes something
else: the purely digital and entirely manmade, a reflection on cinematic
creation and commercial genericness rather than an image of a particular
specimen. What is the 'original' version of an image meant to recall –
all images and none in particular? What is the 'authentic' version of
a simulation? In various ways over the past ten years the very idea of
the original, already degraded by twentieth-century theories of lateral
hierarchies and appropriation – the simulacrum, the Pictures critique,
etc. –, has lost purchase. What is 'authentic' in a situation where all
context is contingent or, more likely, absent?

It is against this backdrop that Martin started the project *UR Feeling*, which
began as a curated show at the Camden Arts Centre 2013 and which he

has since made into a film with two dancers, Nissa Nishikawa and Martin
Tomlinson. The film takes the premise of trying to find collective memory:
questioning whether there is an 'ur-feeling', a way to sense something
that has been lost, or a feeling of origins that persists despite the shift
into this world of the simulacrum. Describing feeling as a 'scaffolding',
Martin uses architectural metaphors to explore this condition, wondering,
for example, whether the tangled Victorian lanes behind St. Paul's can
be felt after the razing and subsequent makeover of Paternoster Square,
adjacent to the cathedral, or whether walking into the new Foyle's on
Charing Cross Road, one can feel the echoes of Central St Martins College
of Art & Design, which used to occupy the site (and whose cachet Foyle's
has been happy to capitalise on). *UR Feeling*, that is, cuts against the grain
of the push towards surface, context collapse or extreme presentness.
It positions itself in a state of after, looking back, and questions whether
we can still access the origins – the authenticities – that used to be.

For Martin, this notion of authenticity has inhered in objects and
sound rather than bodily movement. Throughout his work the objects
he has chosen to focus on have been domestic ones – doorknobs,
chairs, bookshelves – echoing the notion of the house as a repository
of memory. Objects never quite seem 'old' in his work, with their stylish
gleam of |recent postmodernism, but Martin's voiceovers are careful
to give them the full history of their production – to make sure the viewer
knows the facts about these ordinary objects. In *UR Feeling*, by contrast,
there is no voiceover, and the dancers refuse all notion of context, with
their anytime-since-the-70s haircuts and T-shirts and jeans: the very
triumph of postmodernism, perhaps, but also the very beast that they
mitigate against. The film is careful to perform the lack of periodisation
implied as well as the idea of pastiche itself. The clothes the performers
wear are Bruce Nauman-like. The black-and-white, bare bones style
of the *mise-en-scène* is Judson School-esque. Tomlinson's haircut and
bearing is 70s-ish. The high-production values of the shooting make
the film immediately appealing, but also anodyne, like a well-made Gap
ad or a campaign conceived in Shoreditch. This gives one, on the level
of production, not much to hold onto.

And this is the condition the performers work against: physically
struggling to find – or to mimic – some reverberation of a setting or
built environment that predates its re-representation. The mighty Thames,
perhaps, or the sense of being lost within a narrow alley that doesn't let
in the light. Visceral, heart-fluttering feelings that come in a world that
can be genuinely frightening at times. Not 'Disneyfied', that is, which is
the term of choice for architectural creations that take as their origin –
and assiduously, eerily, reconstruct – the cultural idea of things rather
than being grown organically: Times Square in New York after Giuliani;

the rebuilt centre of Münster after World War II; the Dresden Frauenkirche, likewise rebuilt; even the Madinat Jumeirah in Dubai – ironically for a city which is commonly believed to have been created in the last 40 years, making the whole thing close to an a-memorial site – a hotel and shopping complex that re-creates a version of a forbidden garden of Arabia. The Madinat, down the road (highway) from one of Dubai's manmade 'palm tree' peninsulas, is extremely popular for locals and tourists alike. Writing this – as I happen to be – from the UAE makes one keenly aware of the social and political valences of postmodernism and a lack of memory of the past: it is a country whose main mode of self-expression seems to be Orientalist pastiche (how much this is taken as authentic Arabia, and by whom, I don't know) which runs alongside a government-mandated policy of Emiratisation – that, for the moment, involves employing Westerners to train up local Emiratis. It's an import / export economy in many ways. Like the Madinat, 'Disneyfied' implies the commercial motivations behind these reconstructions: Gap ads are good bands *retourned*.

To perform this sense of an unseen history bearing down – the performers shake, drop, collapse – Nishikawa studied Butoh dance techniques in Japan that focus on this very movement. The internal torsion, the constant movement, the mode of extreme self-possession signals both repression and release – containing poles is key to their choreography, as it has been to Martin's practice. In the same way that Freud's notion of the uncanny held together two opposites – the familiar and the dreadfully alien – the dancers here seem to push back and forth against, or rather to simply reverberate within, a situation of counterparts. They dredge up the basic fear at the heart of forgotten memory: the rush of joy at a memory regained, and the horror that something could be so entirely forgotten.

UR Feeling is thus not only about the theoretical notion of pastiche but explores two bodies inhabited by it, in the way that reverb is not only heard but felt, echoing the way that one of the greatest anxieties provoked by the new digital environment is the loss of one's body – the spectre of immateriality. Online we are only eyes and brains; our avatars, like Martin's frog, exist, being 'us' without any of the physicality that makes us. The title of *UR Feeling* stems from the German prefix 'ur-', meaning something that came from the very beginning (the question of origins), as well as text-speak for 'your' – your feeling, something that is at risk of being lost as 'feeling' becomes something only emotional and not sensational, in the stricter sense of the word.

In *UR Feeling* this attention to the physical side of things underlines where the loss of authenticities is felt – the chokehold on experience that the dancers seem trapped within – and makes the film mesmerising, impossible to turn away from. It is not just their skill as dancers but the sense of both violence and calm they contain within themselves. What would manifestations of collective memory look like, *UR Feeling* asks? Would they be violent eruptions, or quiet murmurings that get in under the skin?

The digital cinema theorist Vivian Sobchack wrote an essay called 'What My Fingers Knew' about her tactile response to the film *The Piano*. The essay forms part of a wider theoretical movement called 'embodied spectatorship', which aims to expand the sensational experience of watching film beyond simply retinal exposure, i.e. to include bodily responses as part of theoretical spectatorship – think horror films, pornography, or even romantic comedies: spectatorship felt in the gut or that give you chills. It also, not incidentally, aims to enlarge the terms of scholarship to better assess films that do not rely as much on the visual. It is argued that films of the Third World or its diaspora conjure up smells and feelings more than simply sight, and embodied spectatorship allows the analysis of these films to not simply be reduced to Western heuristics. But Sobchack's essay, which argues that her fingers could recognise the initial, blurry image of the film's protagonist's fingers before her eyes or mind could ('tactile foresight'), for me ran up against one crucial problem: my fingers, like the rest of me, were totally bored during *The Piano*. They didn't 'know' much except the passing of time. Indeed, although we watch films and go about everyday life with our bodies, the subjective dimension of bodily response makes it extremely difficult to theorise or make generalisations about these experiences: it is a sited, sighted response. In cutting against the absence of context, by locating bodies as the place where memories might be felt, *UR Feeling* runs up against an age-old problem: how does the 'one' access the 'we'? How seriously, moreover, can we take Martin's premise that these dancers might represent eruptions of forgotten currents?

To me, writing from a new and vastly different, hot country in January, the dancer's movements seem more European than they did in December, when I watched them with a scarf around my neck in south London after enduring a massive transportation failure getting there. That is, despite the Japanese roots of Nishikawa's training, and despite the universal aspirations that are embedded in both the allusion to 'ur-' and in the idea itself of collective memory, they suggest London in all its specificity. They seem, even, a way of keeping oneself warm in a cold climate: think of Danny Fox's underlining of the cold outside and the warm wood he pressed his face against. I don't know why I insisted on writing that Martin calls Dan Fox 'Danny Fox' – though of course I do, and it's because Simon Martin and Dan Fox ('Dan Fox', to me) were two of the first people I met when moving to London, and their interests and background and even mode of conversation were so new as to be utterly alien. They were steeped in a culture I had no knowledge of, and their deep familiarity with various subcultures (says the one coming from the hegemonic New York City) was different to anything I'd seen before; it opposed the idea of a lateral hierarchy in its very mode of affiliation. In retrospect, their concerns – style, expression, reference – are not only hallmarks of Martin's chosen era of exploration but national characteristics that inflect so many of the UK's best contemporary artists. (Just a read through of Fox's essay proves how deft he is at manoeuvring around these ideas. Americans writing about postmodernism will sap the blood from your veins – imagine someone British saying something as didactic as Fox's Whit Stillman quote.) The -esque, -ish, -likenesses that *UR Feeling* conjures are part of a particular tradition: the obsession with surface actually speaks about a deeper mode of engagement with art and literature. This is not to reduce *UR Feeling* to a typical 'British' artwork, a kind of contemporary-art Mike Leigh, but to suggest that it is related to context in ways more subtle and rooted than at first appears. *UR Feeling* is its own context, a symptom of the idea itself as much as a performance of it – and it allows memory to be freely, questionably collective.

'Causality theories are preoccupied with explaining things away, with demystification. A theory of cause and effect shows you how the magic trick is done. But what if something crucial about causality resided at the level of the magic trick itself?'[1]

'If *eye* be a spirit free to choose, 4 its own share, What case of flesh or rock *eye* pleazed 2 wear. Am be papier-mâché, Mahogany. Spunk ov tree?'[2]

Diffuse light bounces off the 200gsm polymer page of a well-thumbed magazine. An *ORCH5 sample* echoes in the endless shadow-void of its composite black CMY. A dream-thing.

Ettore Sottsass' 'Carlton' polychrome room divider is a collective hallucination from 1981. While it resembles a totem, it is disdainful of the totemic. Denaturalised and discursive, the Memphis design group was all busy representational surfaces rather than functional 'depth'. It coquettishly flirted with the power of museological artefacts only to make decorative, desublimating puns. After the fall of the Republic of Ubiquitous Dissembling Sublimated Aluminium Woodgrain, it's hard for some to forgive Memphis' shamelessly non-stick skeuomorphism.[3]

It was never going to be easy to destroy its prototype object or escape the magnetic ambience of the social life of such things. The lingering pauses in Simon Martin's 16mm film *Carlton* (2006) nevertheless intimate a temporary annulment of this prototype by arresting its vicarious life. This raises our awareness of, and receptiveness to, the thing's material recalcitrance. Mute and aloof, suspended in dead air, this apparition drifts gently by. No longer hiding behind social relations to neighbouring objects, it is a spectre venturing out of its shy retreat into a long, dry, stringy light.

'The explanation emerges once the description is saturated.'[4]

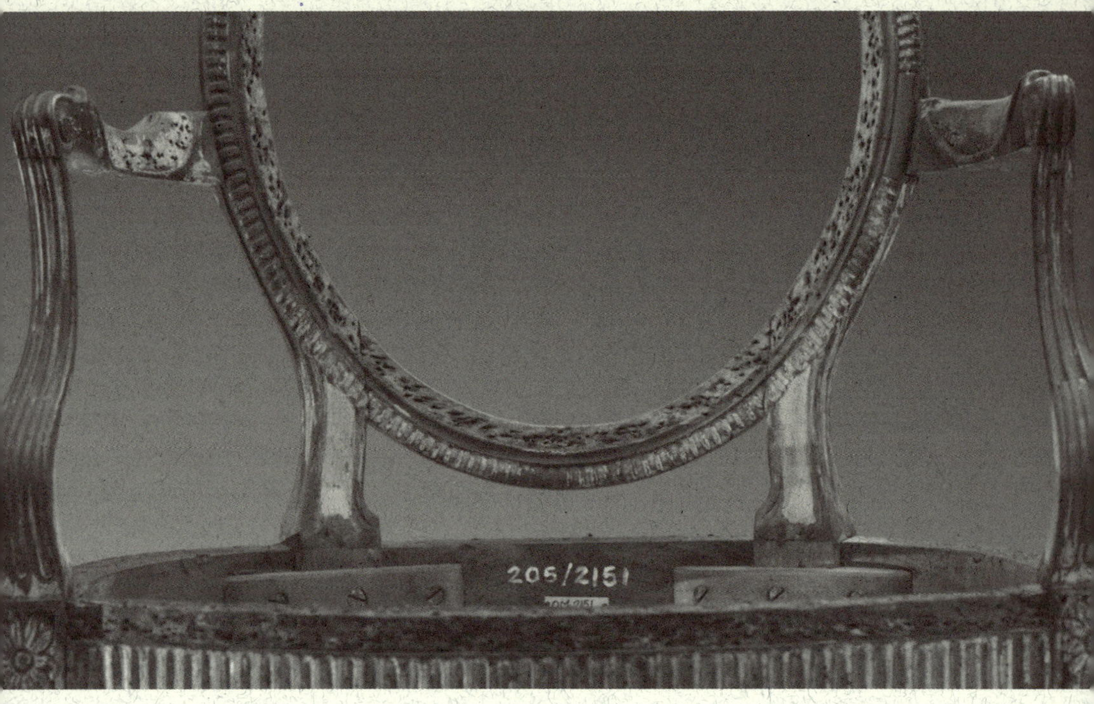

44 Martin's deadpan narrators oscillate between 'thin' and 'thick' description.[5]
In each performance, a series of artefacts (model, shelf, chairs, gnomes,
stool, sculpture) slowly unfold as thin descriptions separate finite material
dimensions from a dense *demi-glace*. Once a range of ingredients has been
unstuffed, layered interpretations and cultural speculation glaze and amplify
the artefacts' aleatory potential.

'Thick' description in *Louis Ghost Chair* (2012) situates a Louis XV chair
amidst transformations in manufacturing that lie between the French
Revolution and the present, a period in which the rise of mass production
helped to usurp not only the artisanal but the *ancien régime* that was its
chief patron. Cornstarch thickens this stock into a slurry. The Louis XV
chair is antique sentiment risen from the ashes of Herculaneum and Pompeii
to furnish the *ancien régime*; reanimation of the antique activated classical
materials in unexpected ways. As it transpired, 'antique sentiment' was also
the root of a revolutionary republicanism that levelled everything in its path.
The Louis XV chair is an avenging, regicidal zombie. The narrator whisks
this starchy mixture, fixing our attention firmly upon the kinetic, reciprocal
relationships between extrasomatic artefacts and human bodies, emphasising
the anchoring of social relations in quantifiable material processes.

Then something else speaks. The sound of a saw cutting wood. Fine rivulets.
Nonrecurring patterns. The tapping of a hammer. This is thin description:

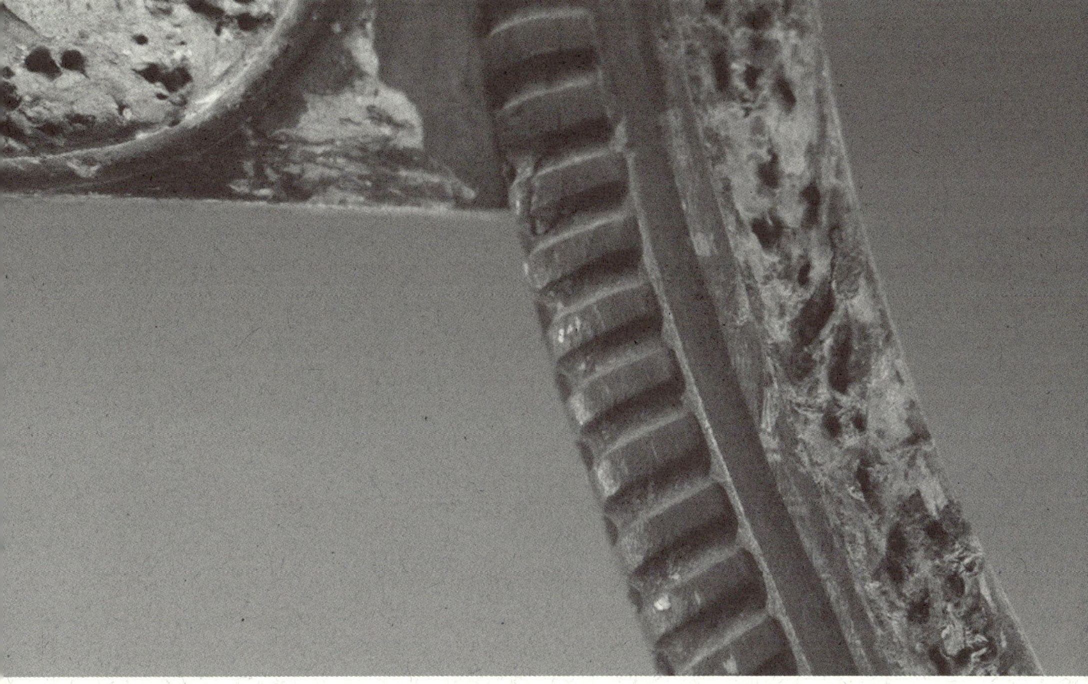

the artisanal presented as 'information', knowledge bereft of experience,
stuff awaiting analysis. We are given slight pause to stare blankly at floating
images of the Louis XV chair isolated and retreating in an amorphous
mise-en-scène.

The chair soliloquises. Close-ups reveal the bruises of wear-and-tear, the
chair's patina unfolding upon us, at the very least, that it has considerable
experience. The camera hovers over a rich and varied social life about
which we are invited to speculate:

> 'In doing the biography of a thing, one would ask questions similar to
> those one asks about people: what, sociologically, are the biographical
> possibilities inherent in its "status" and in the period and culture, and
> how are these possibilities realised?'[6]

This chair's biography would certainly include the narrator's focus on
its affordances, *menuisier* and manufacture. Every mark a remark. This
cherished chair is singular; it invites gossip on the unique life history that
has contributed to its current appearance. Its embryonic development
extends onto a plateau of 'possibilities'.

Philippe Starck's 'Louis Ghost' armchairs (2002) are a developed species
of clones sporting a homogeneous formal repertoire that encourages

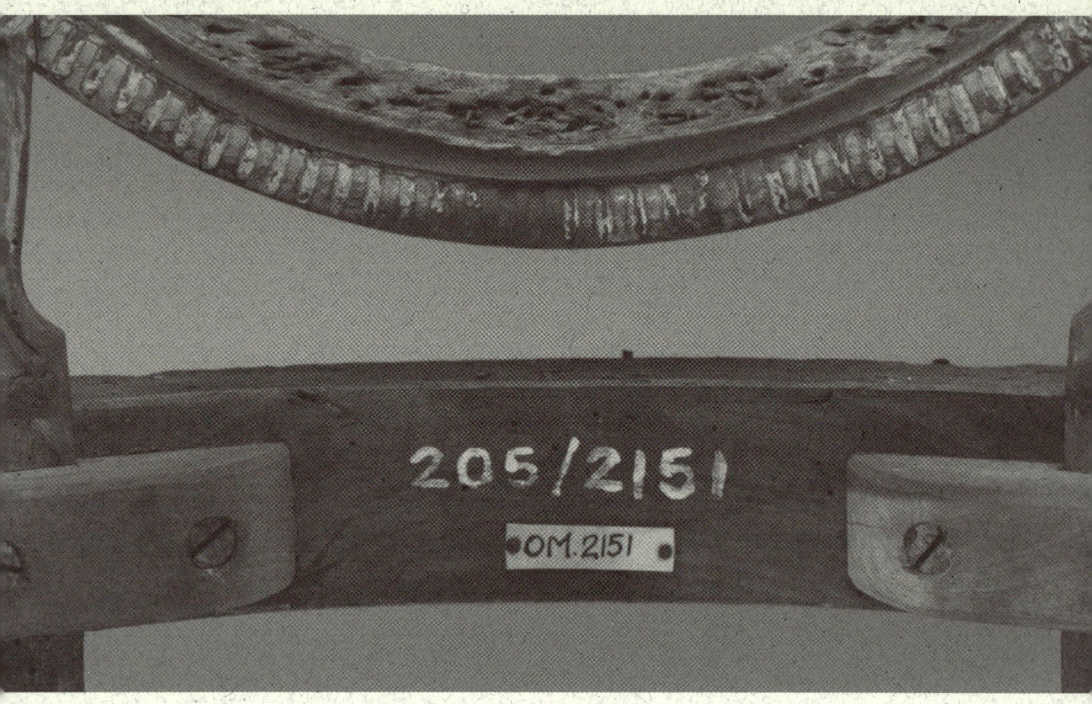

46 speculation on their evolutionary ancestry. Compared to the patina and patois of their ancestors, the box-fresh Ghost armchairs are devoid of exceptional autobiography. As cookie-cutter commodities, they belong to a world of citizens rather than subjects. Louis XV became Citizen Capet. Ye are many – they are few. Things equal among other things. Things 'culturally redefined and put to use.'[7] The lives of other Louis XIV chairs stray and warble in dissembled packets through the congested arteries of history, lasers refracting through a wild field of translucent polycarbonate injected stalks, reassembling to re-upholster antique sentiment.

An oscillatory, cacophonous, and polyvalent cornucopia of memes, 'UR Feeling' arises not from unearthing that which lies beneath, but from straying, warbling and passing through. 'UR Feeling' is sensitivity to the timbre, texture and volume of that which is gestating and vicarious. It involves:

> 'raising artefacts to the status of things that, similarly to organisms, both grow and are grown. To do this, however, requires a change of focus, from the "objectness" of things to the material flows and formative processes wherein they coming into being. It means to think of making as a process of growth, or ontogenesis.'[8]

UR Feeling concerns atmospherics not transparency. Discharges not spectres. Horizons not depth. Transubstantiation not transfiguration.

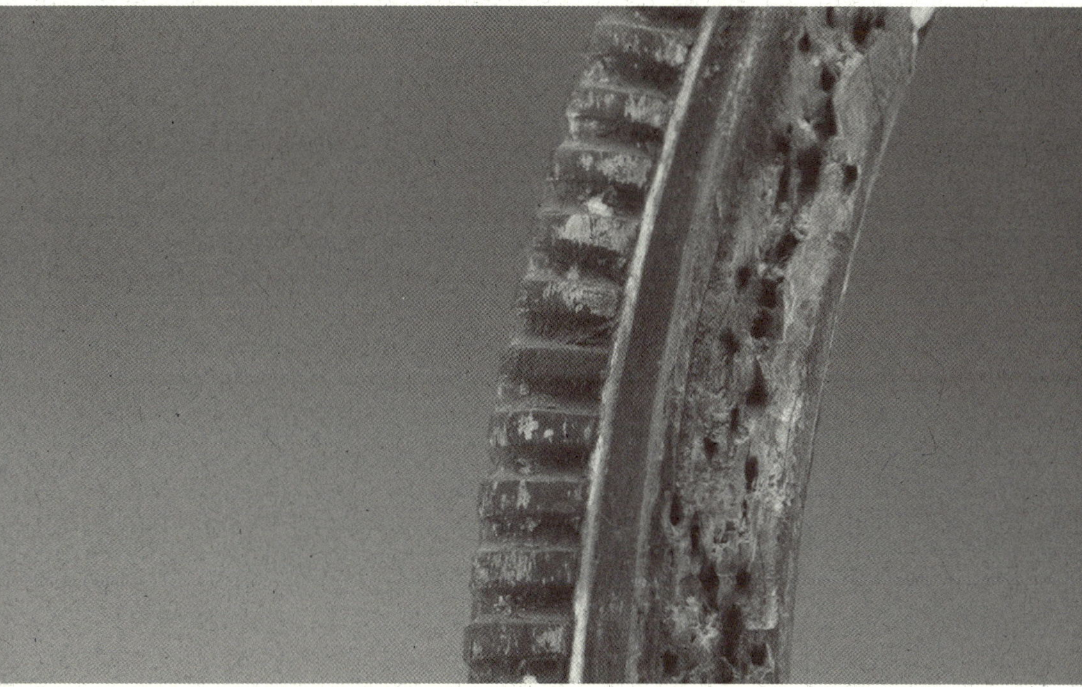

In Luis Buñuel's magic-realist film *The Milky Way* (1969), two vagabonds set out from Paris to traverse the Way of St. James towards Santiago de Compostela. While the journey to Galicia implies a retreat from the modern (industrial metropolis) to the pre-modern (holy retreat), Pierre and Jean's 'pilgrimage' is, in practice, a process without destination. Buñuel arrests time as his incredulous nomads stray via mythical characters, representing the six primary mysteries of medieval Christian faith, and 20th century everymen, the modern pilgrims that Pierre and Jean intend to rob. Before too many tomorrows go by, the vagabonds are drifting and flowing *in medias res*. Their comically dispassionate deconstructions of their magical encounters are countervailed by a reluctance to entirely dispense with the mystery, the 'UR Feeling', of the old articles of faith.

Similarly, Martin's deadpan trilogy takes us on a return journey from a postmodern heretical past-future (*Carlton*) through an expectant modern future-past (*Louis Ghost Chair*) into the black hole of the non-modern middle (*UR Feeling*). When viewed from the perspective of *UR Feeling*, however, the trilogy can be seen as a constellation of relics set adrift in asynchronous time and space. As the depth of field increases and description thins, things temporarily come into sharp focus as discrete (unspeakable) objects before blurring back into the diffuse milky nebulae of hyper-connectivity and interminable speculation. And back again.

1. Timothy Morton, 'Introduction', in *Realist Magic: Objects, Ontology, Causality*,
Open Humanities Press, 2013, p.17. Freely available online at http://hdl.handle.net/2027/
spo.13106496.0001.001

2. Electronic Voice Phenomena received by The Santiago de Compostela Botafumeiro, 6/2/2016.

3. Seen as a pariah from postmodernism, skeuomorphism has recently been hounded out of town
by digital designers such as Apple's Jony Ive.

4. Bruno Latour, 'Technology is Society Made Durable', in J. Law (Ed.) *A Sociology of Monsters:
Essays on Power, Technology and Domination, Sociological Review Monograph*, N°38, 1991, p.129.

5. See Clifford Geertz, 'Chapter 1 Description: Toward and Interpretive Theory of Culture'
in *The Interpretation of Cultures: Selected Essays*, New York: Basic Books, 1973.

6. Igor Kopytoff, 'The Cultural Biography of Things, Commoditization as Process' in Arjun
Appadurai (Ed.) *The Social Life of Things: Commodities in Cultural Perspective*, Cambridge:
Cambridge Studies in Social & Cultural Anthropology, 1988, p.66.

7. ibid., p.67.

8. Tim Ingold, 'Towards an Ecology of Materials' in *Annual Review of Anthropology*, 2012. 41: p.431.

Carlton

part of Cassina's
"project for the image
y". The initiators and
e editor of Domus in
t style of design, as
others. Their state-
he alchemists ex-
gio del Banale, in
rks of art from all
ojan horse of the
s to regard the
ss be taken for
. It's a question
esigner himself
the classicists

as a the
jects of
pattern

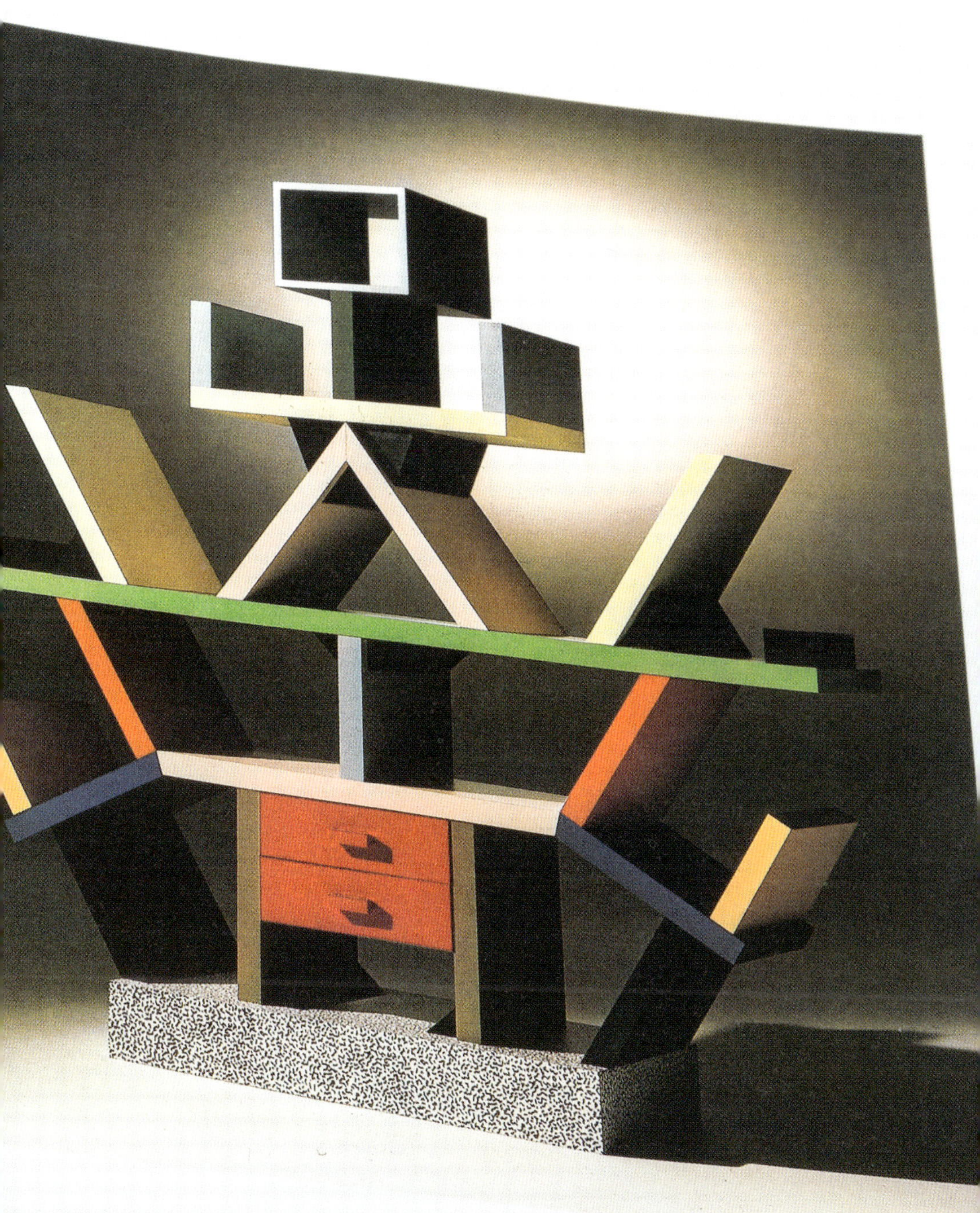

n 1978, Mendini presented "Metamorphoses" of

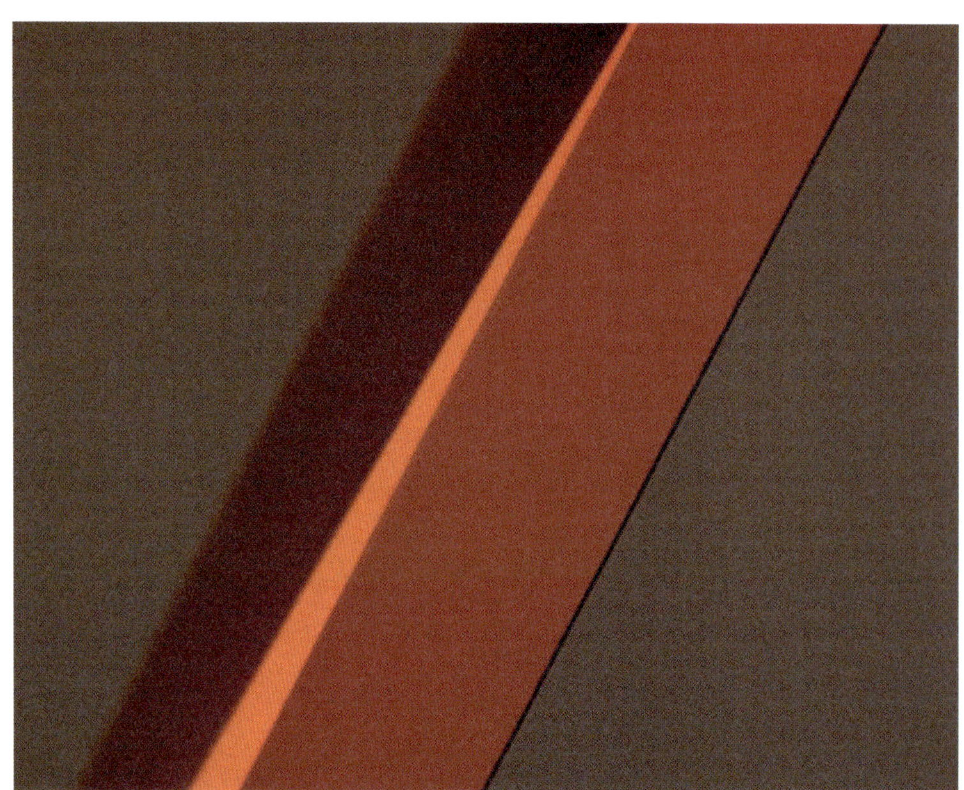

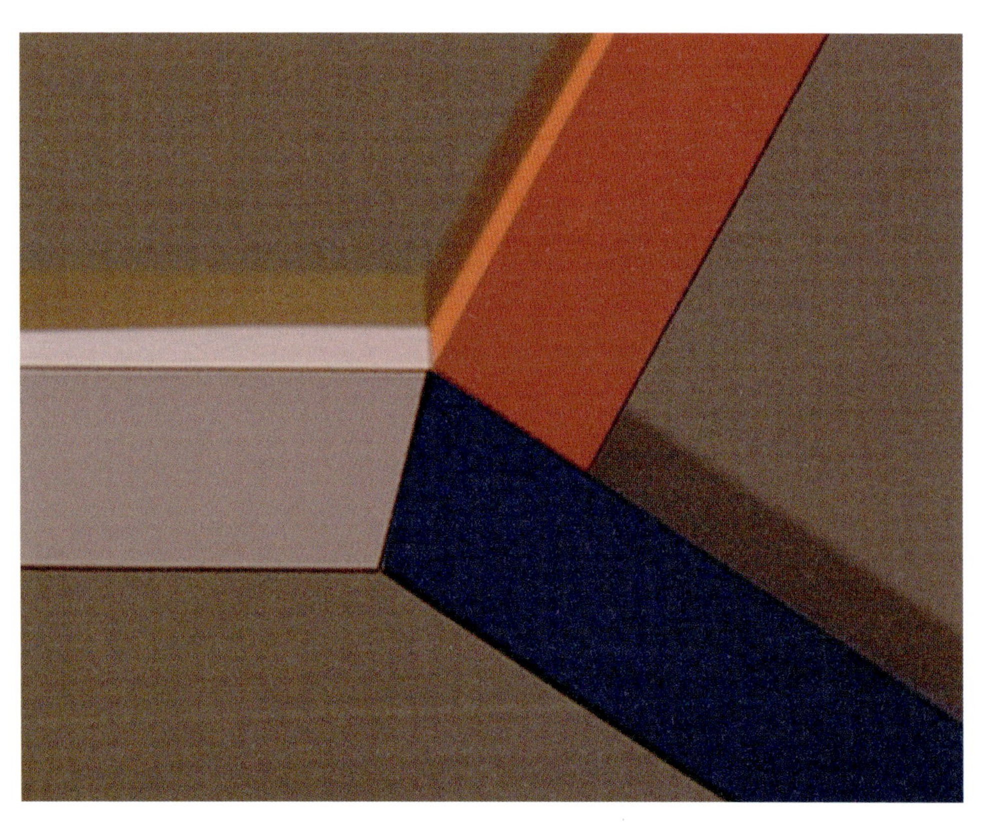

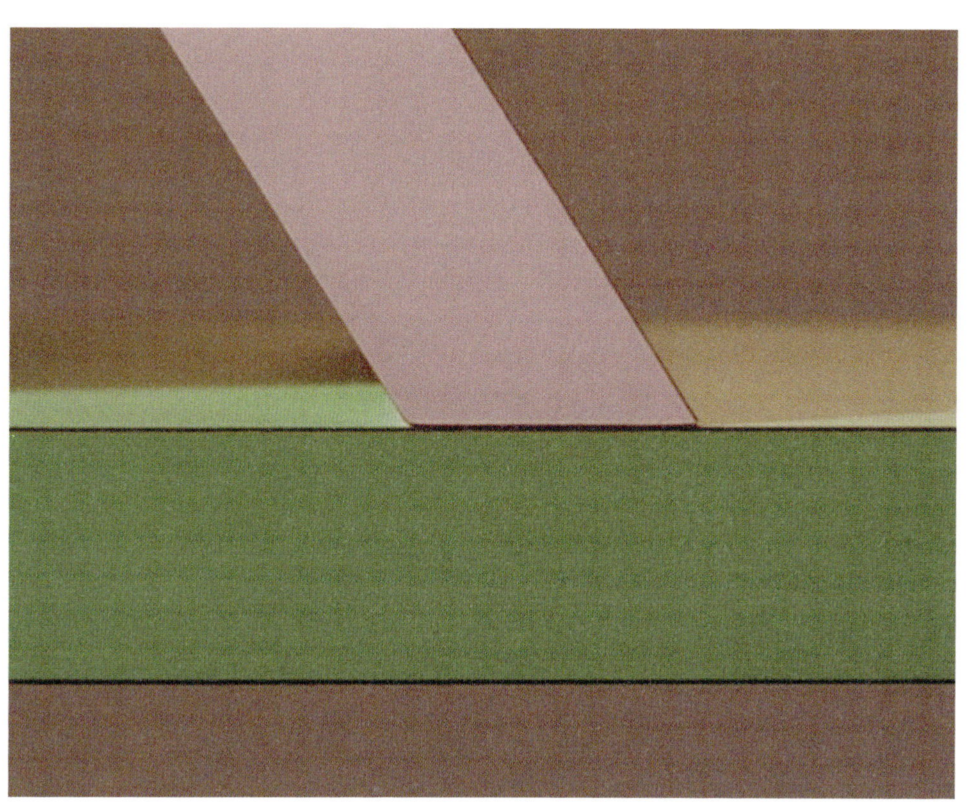

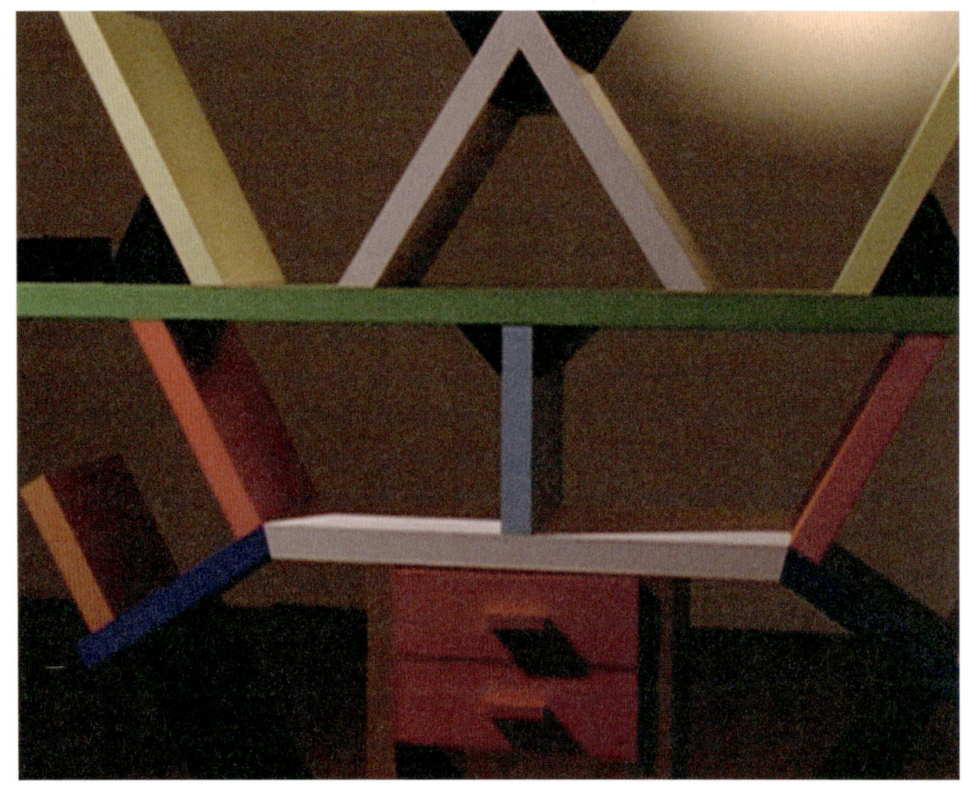

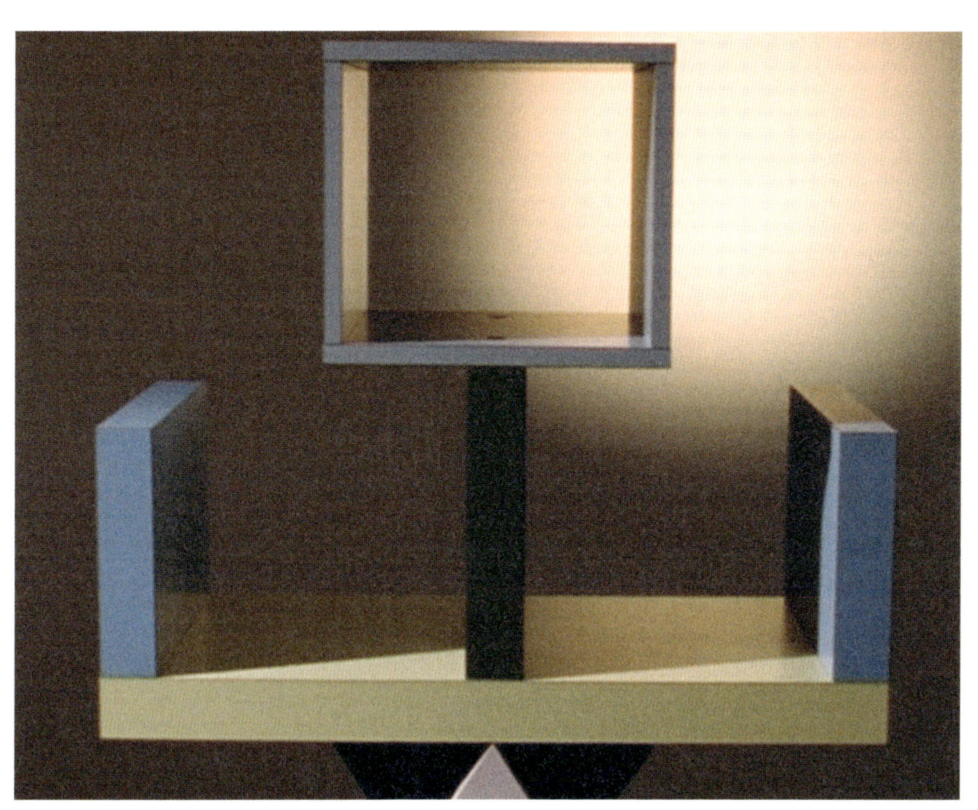

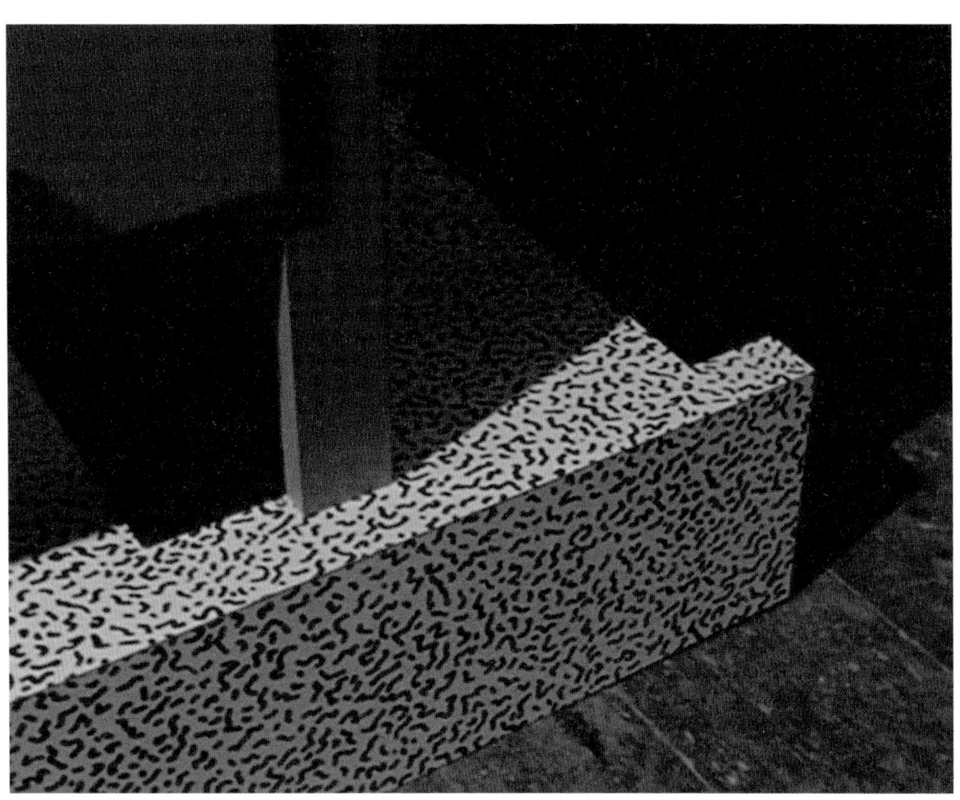

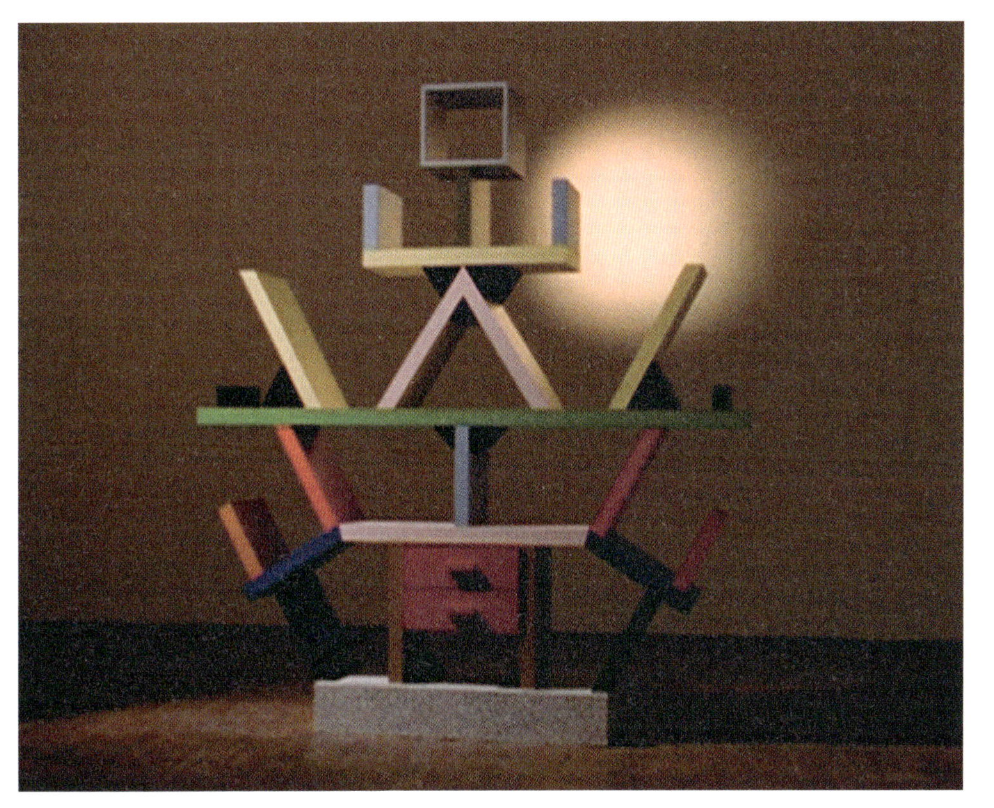

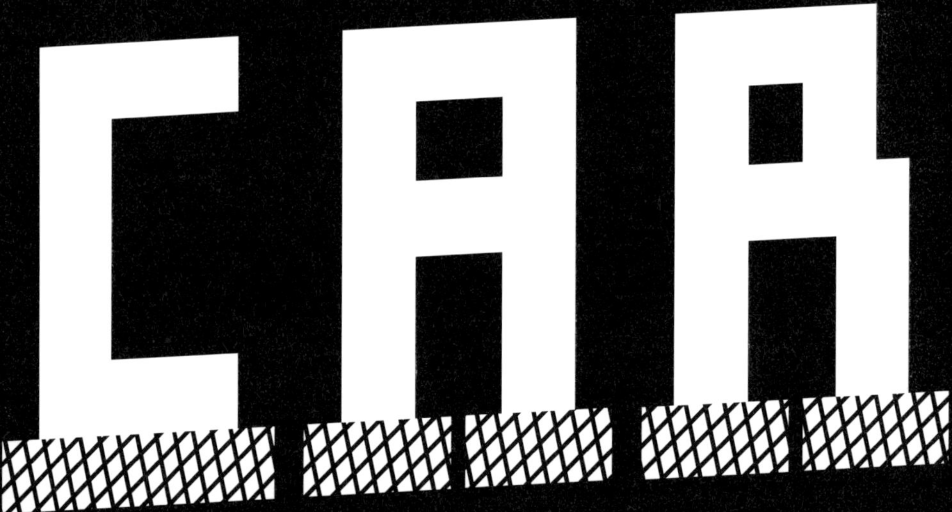

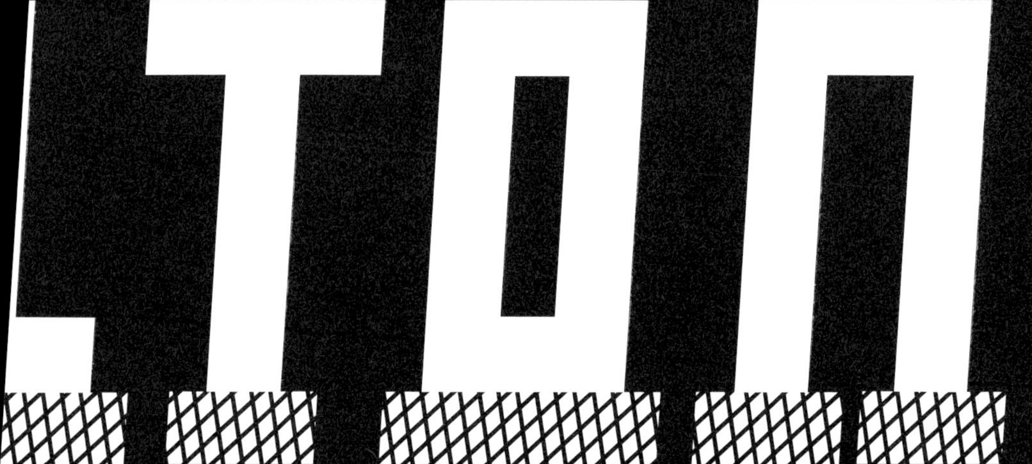

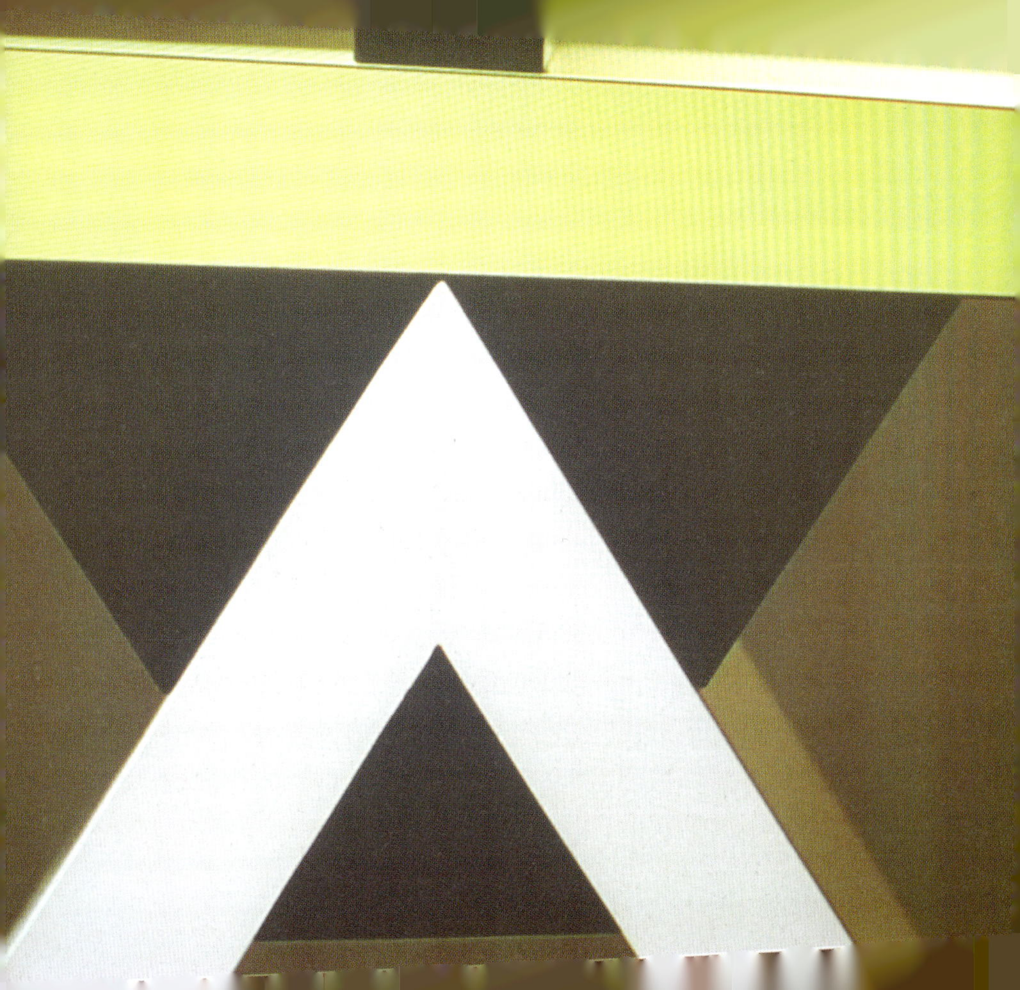

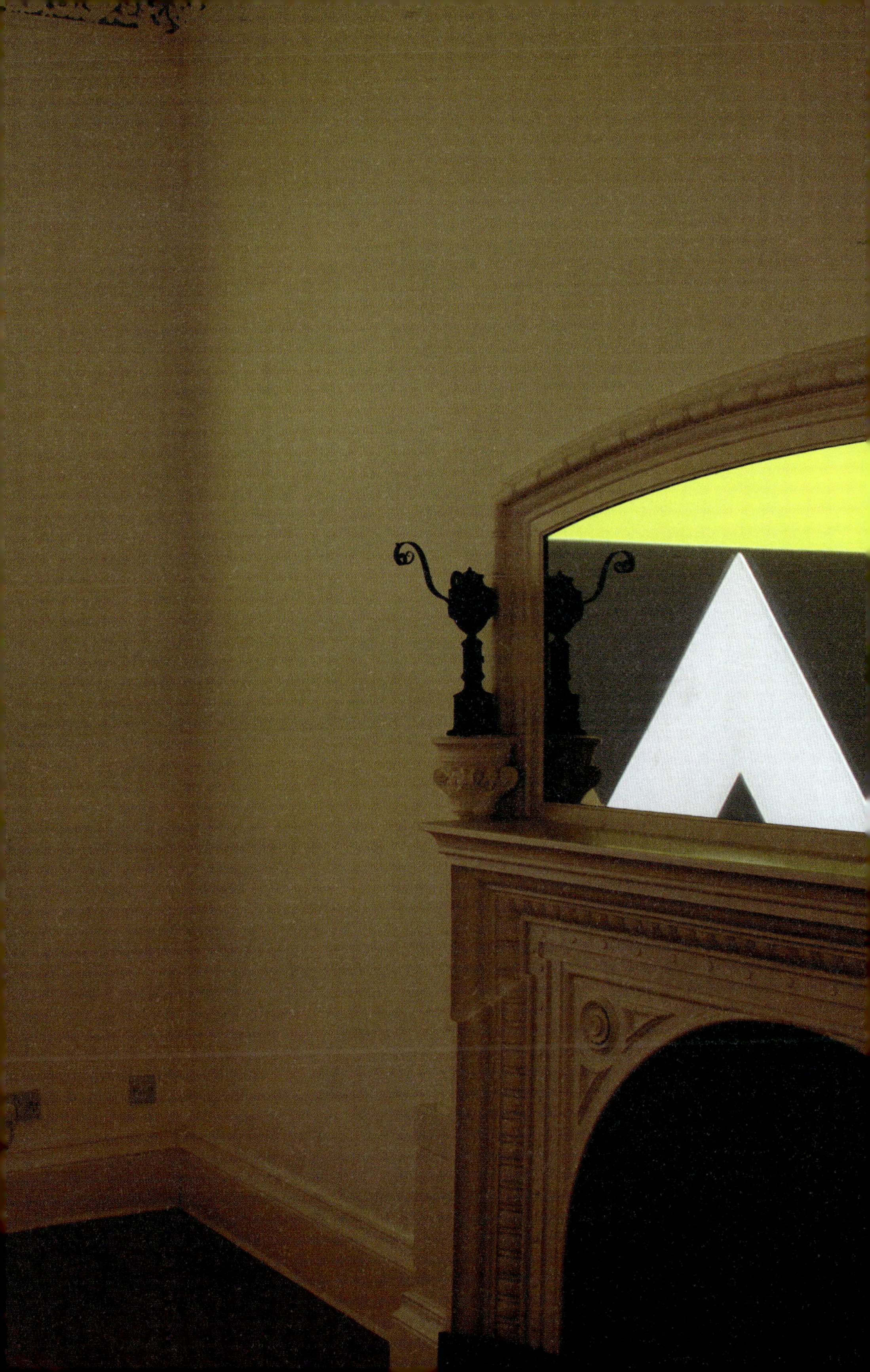

FURNITURE

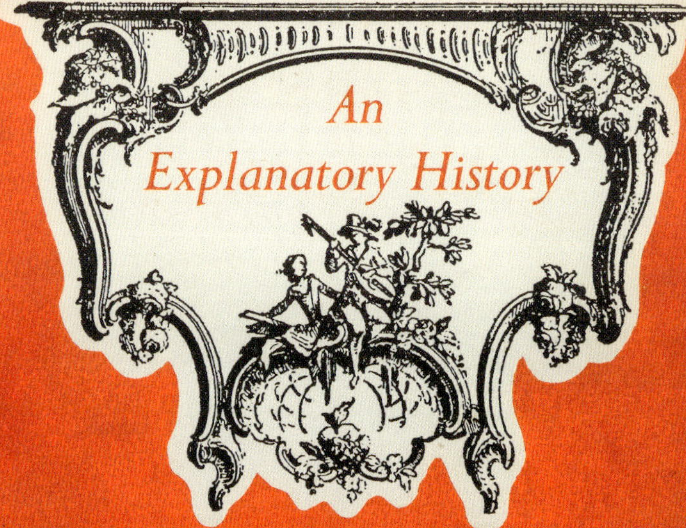

An

Explanatory History

by

David Reeves

FABER

Louis Ghost Chair

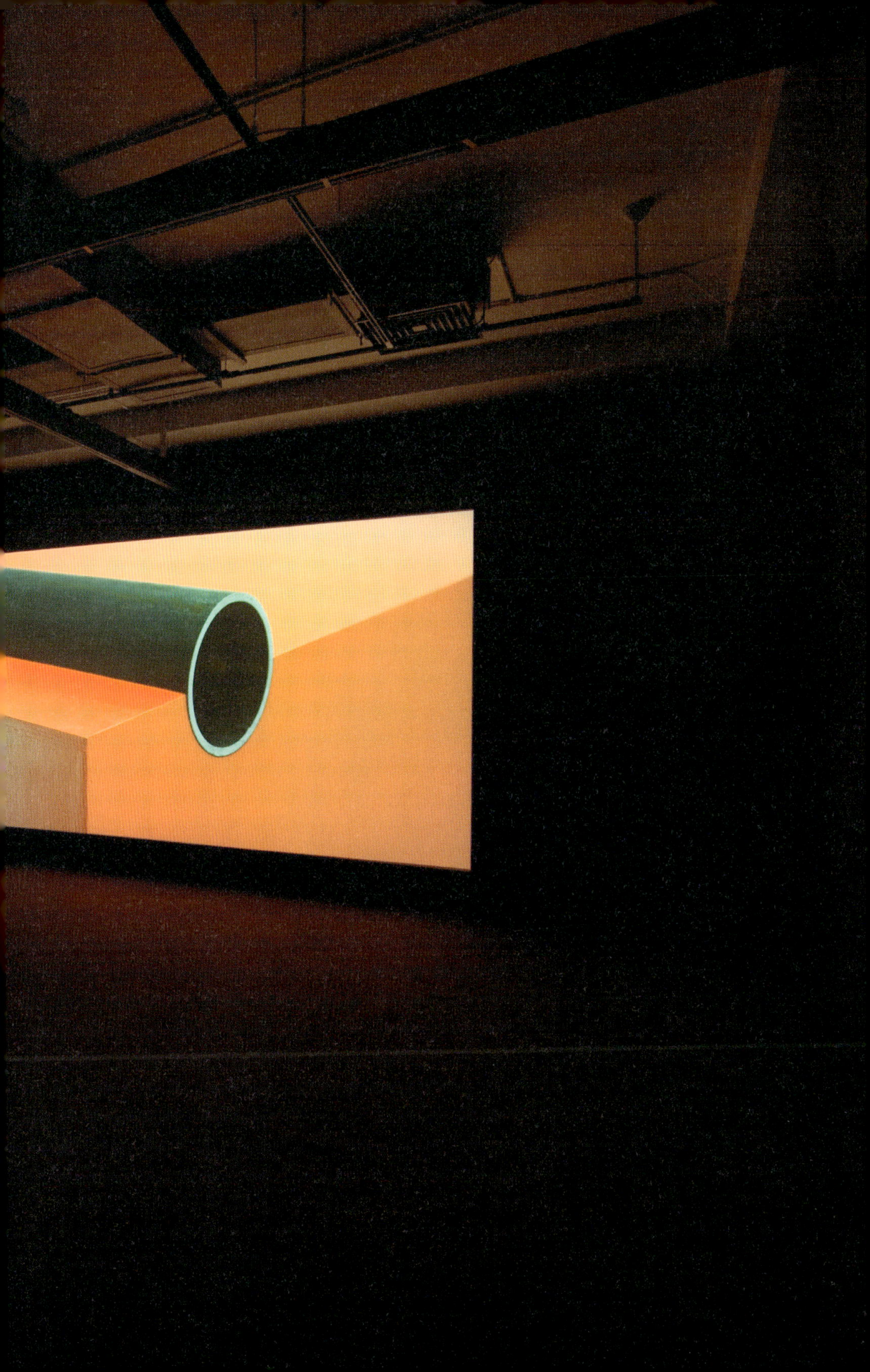

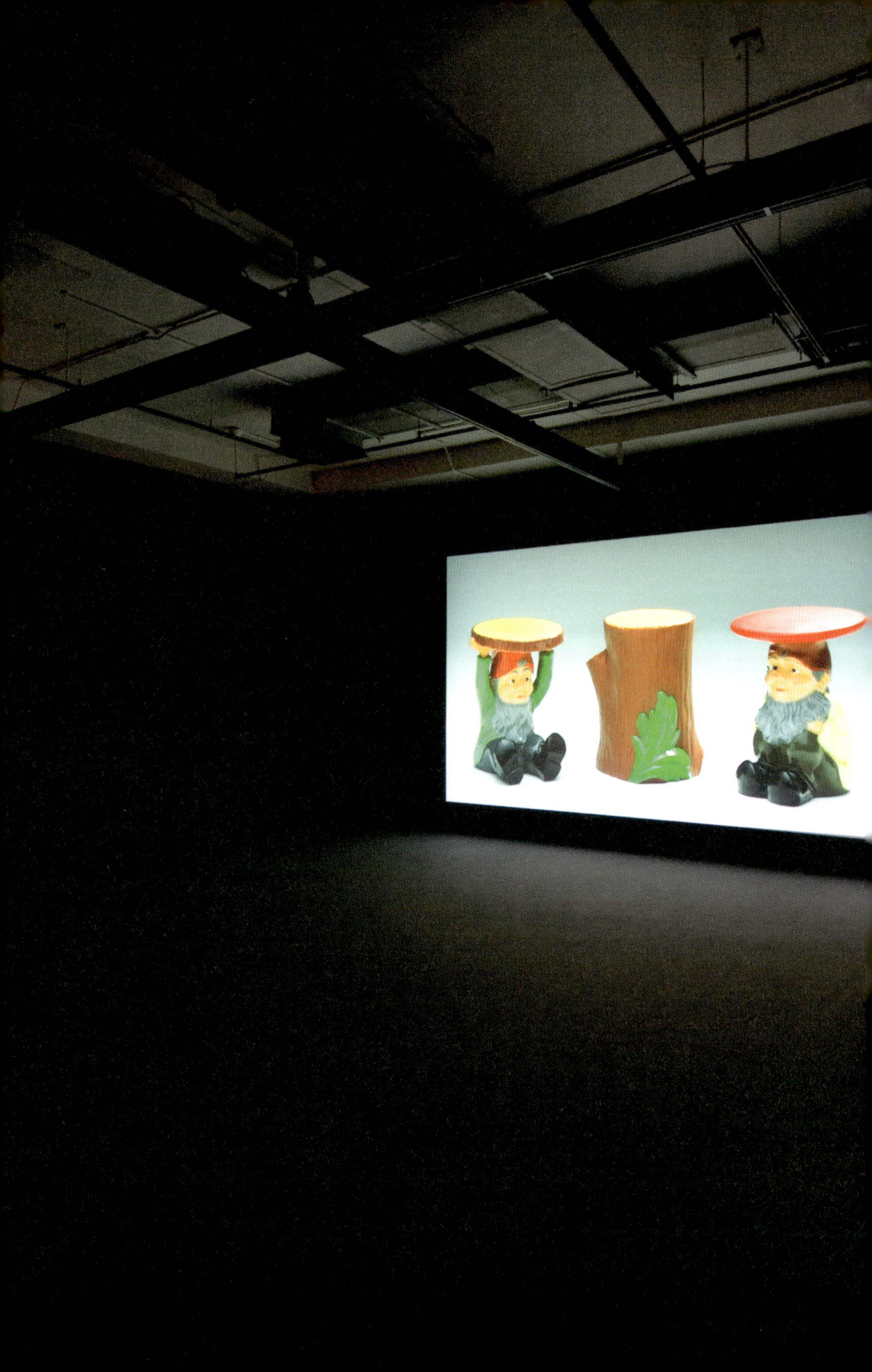

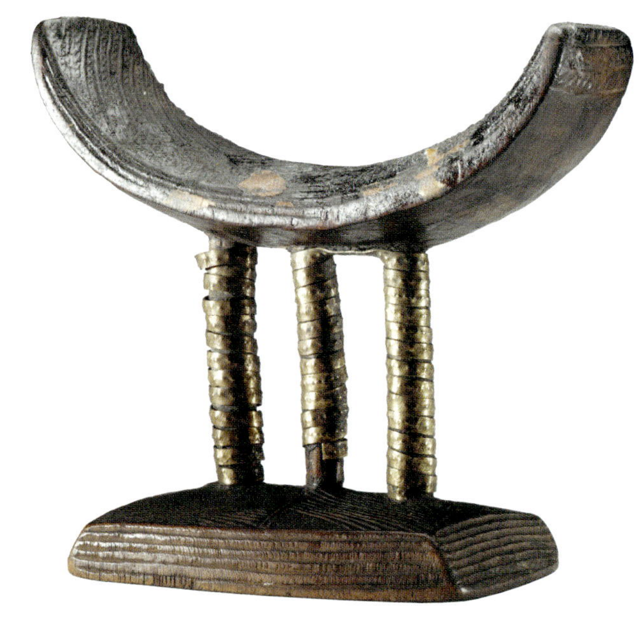

70

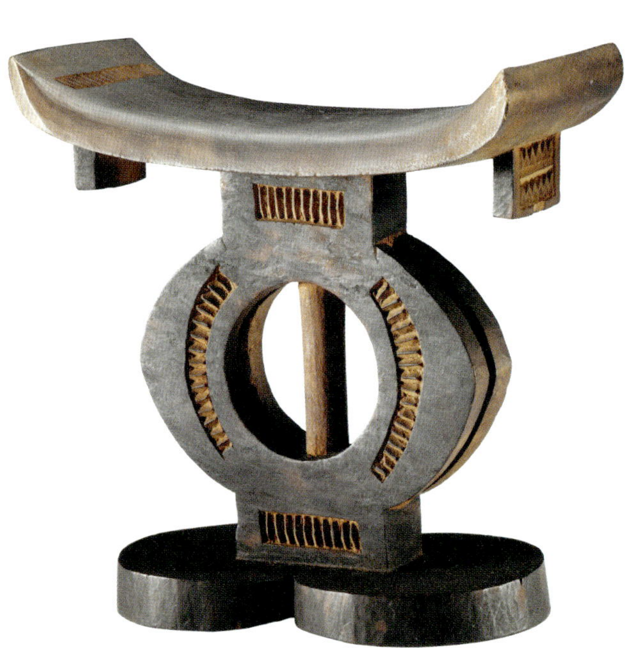

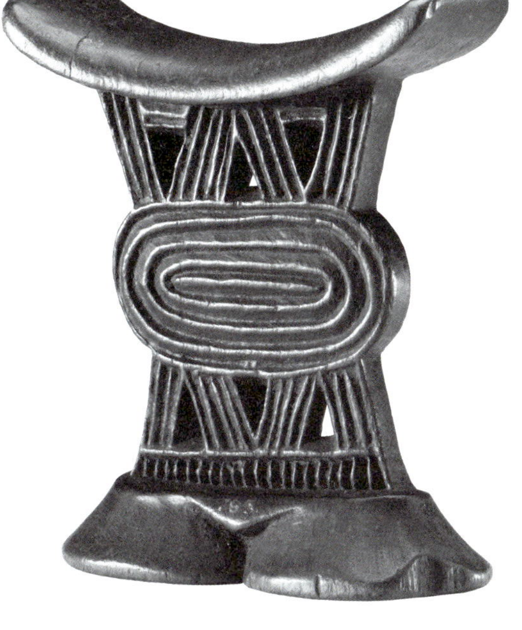

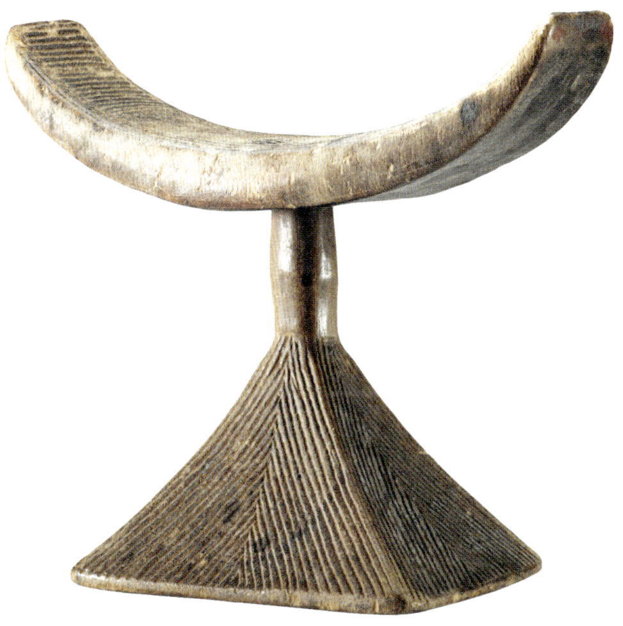

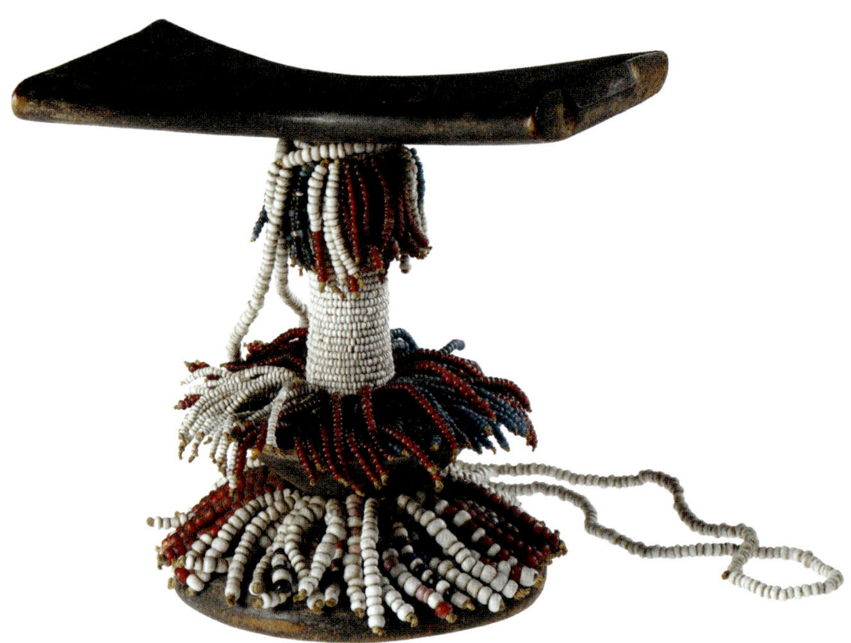

72

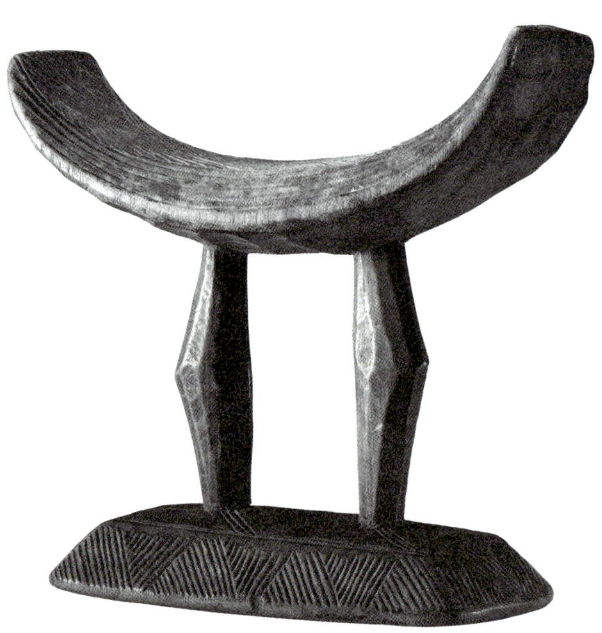

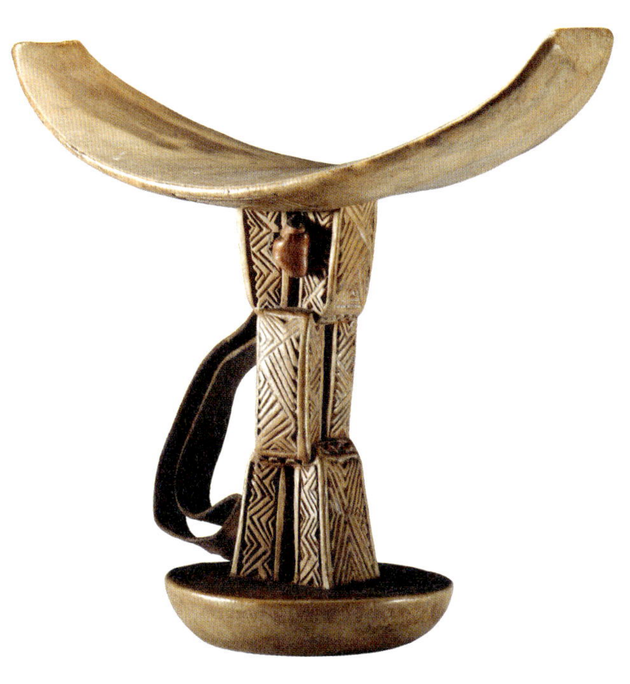

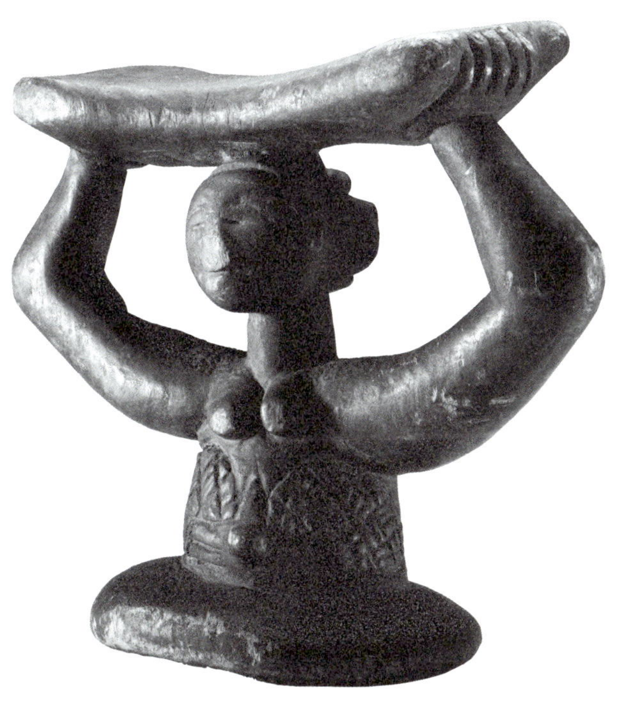

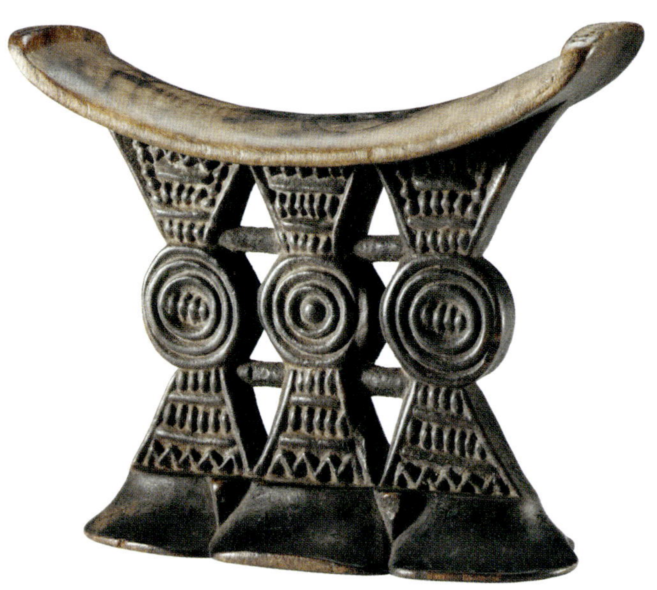

74

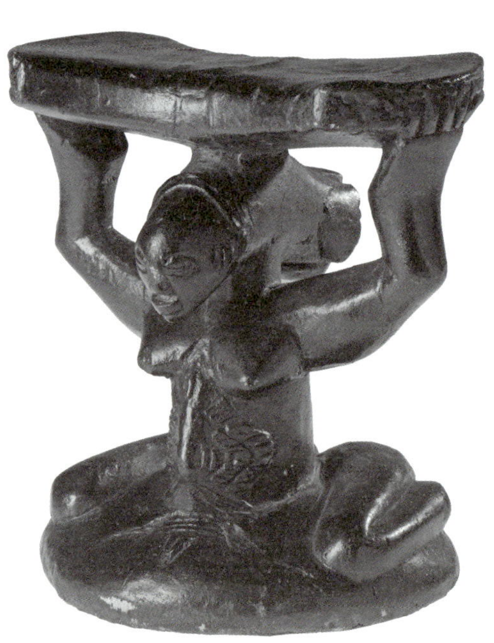

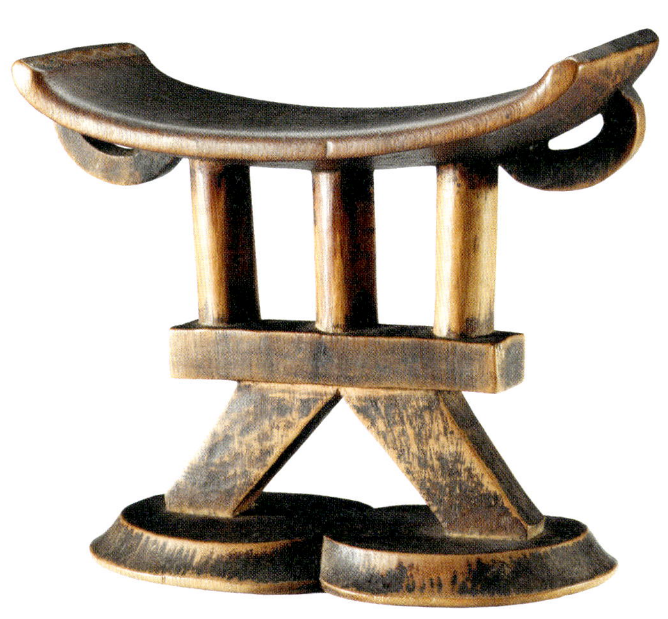

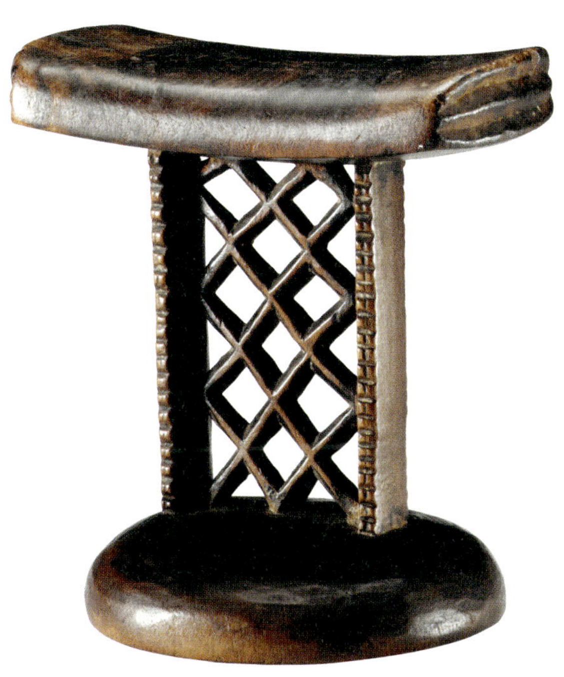

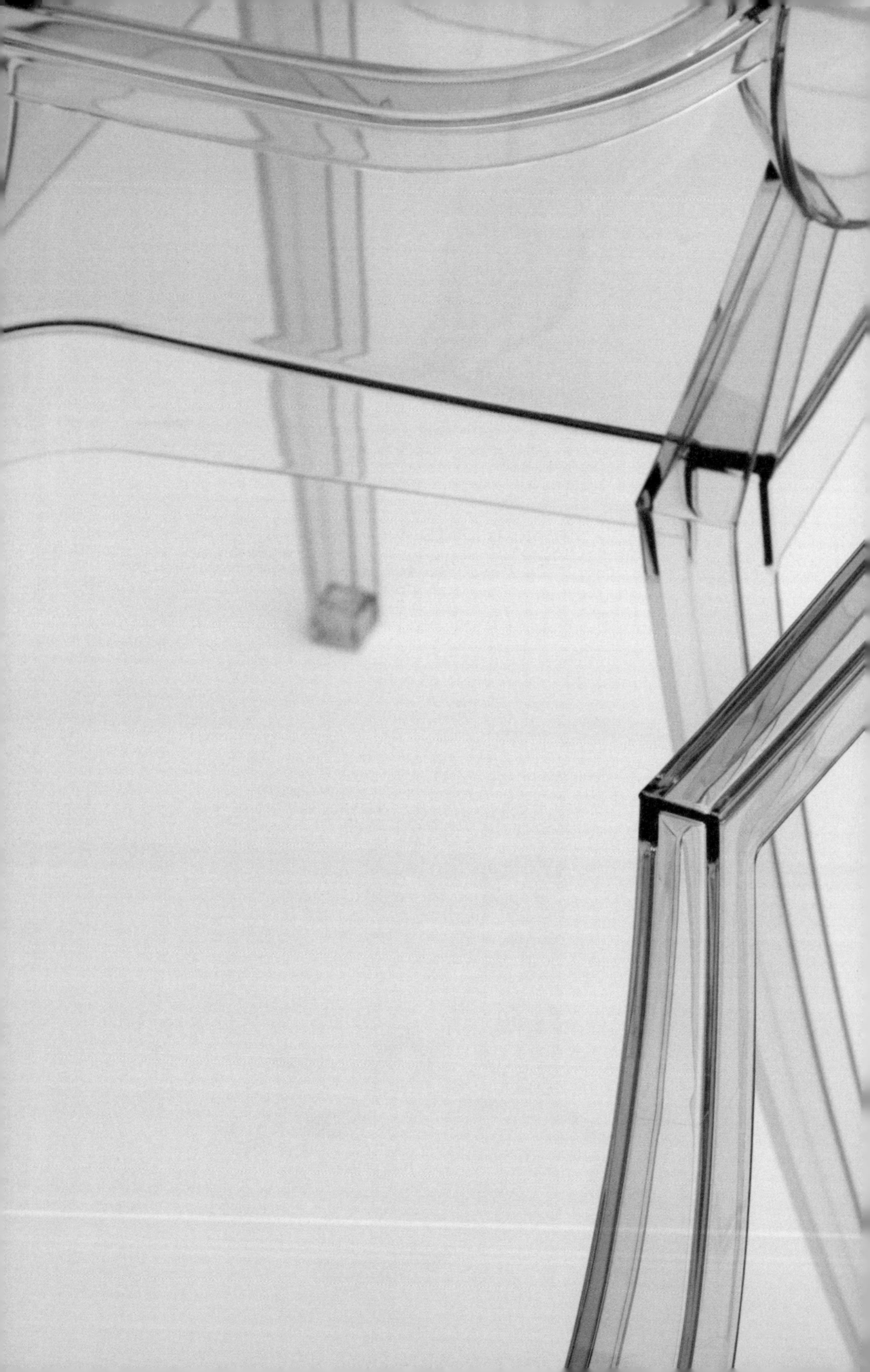

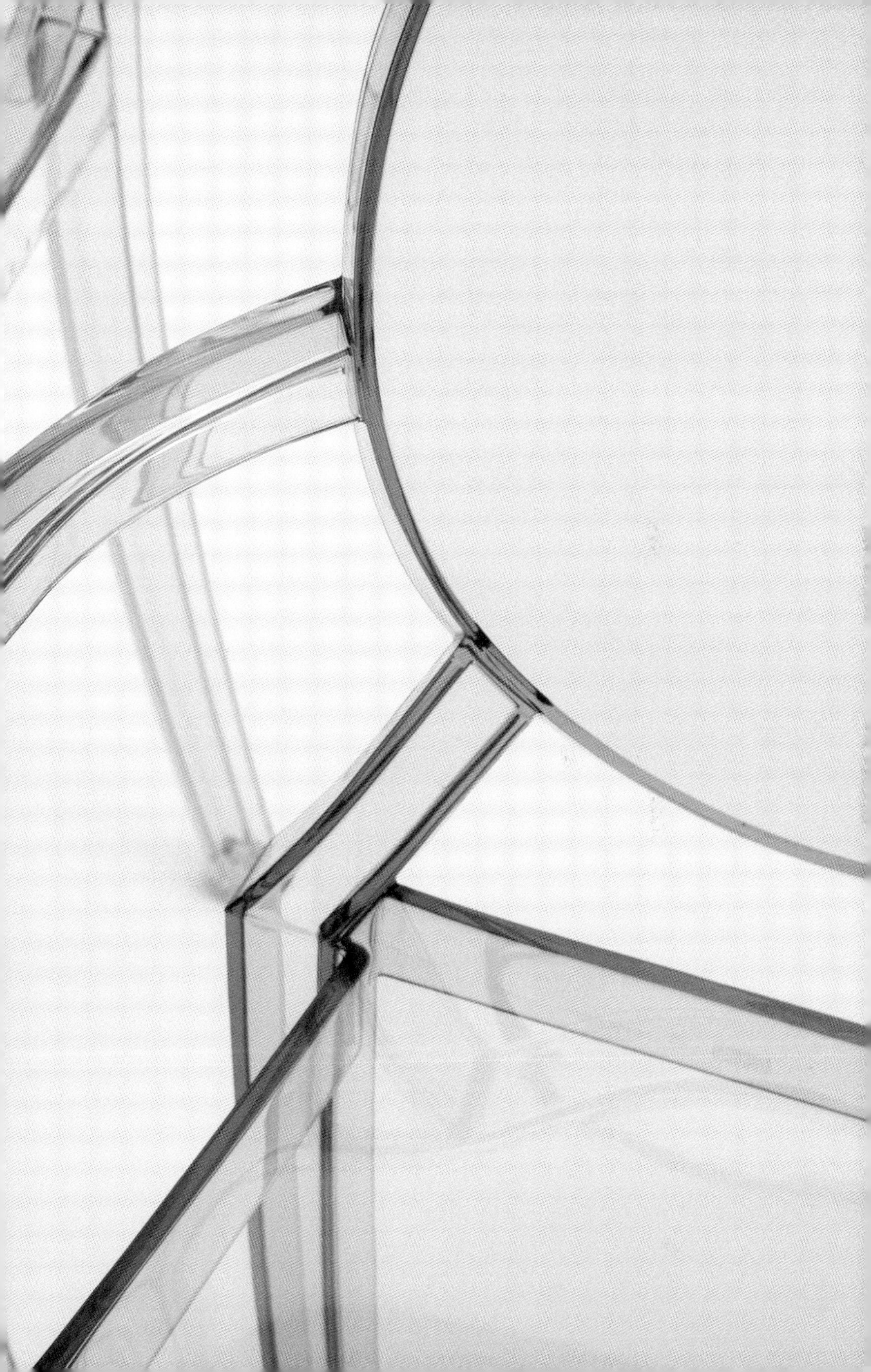

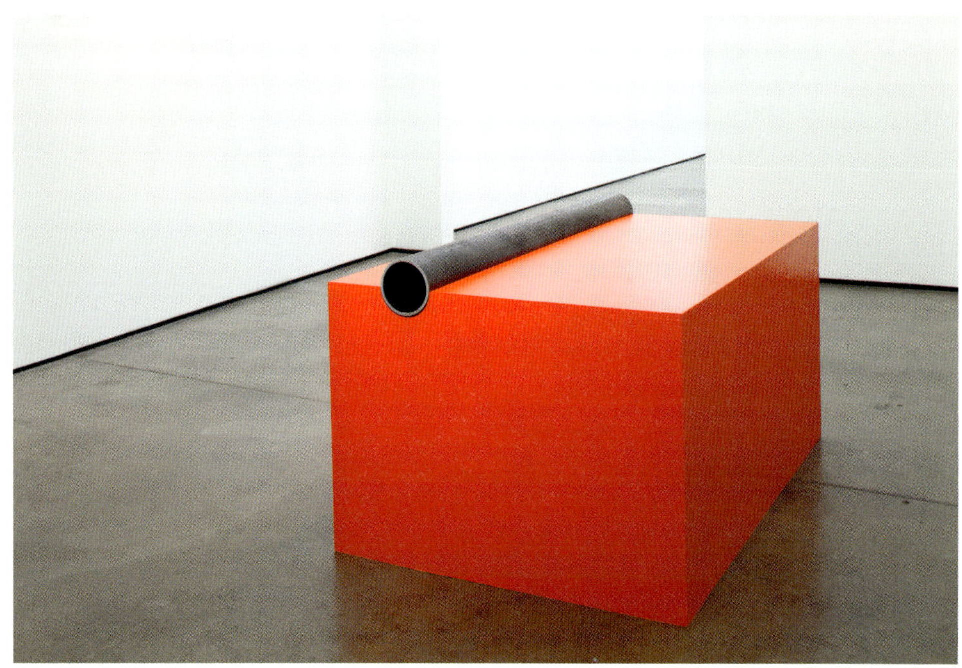

78

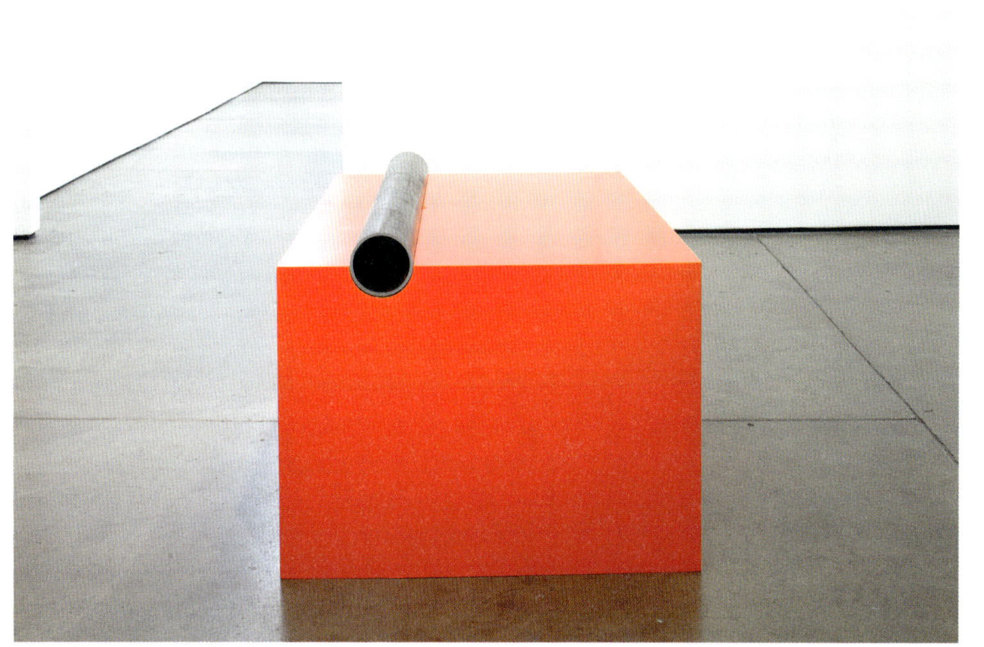

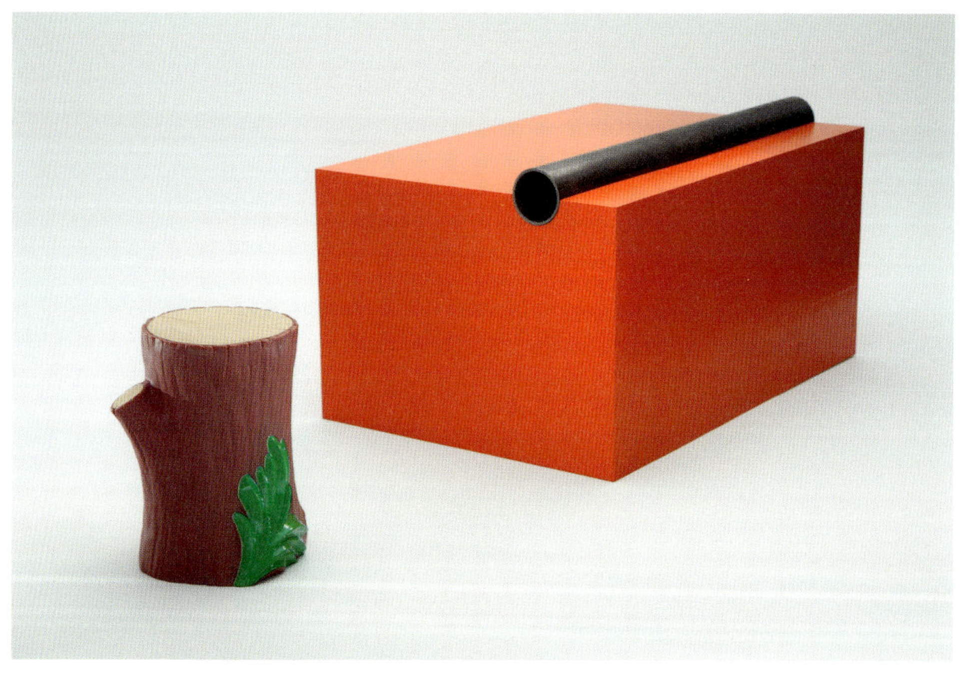

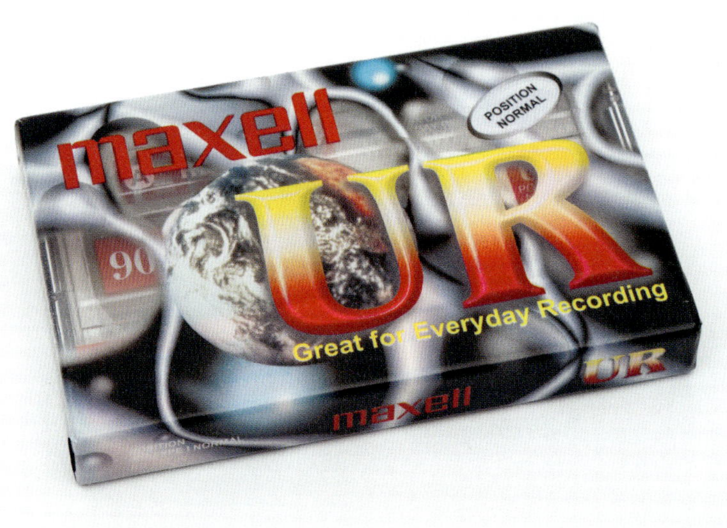
maxell
UR
POSITION NORMAL
90
Great for Everyday Recording
maxell
UR

UR Feeling

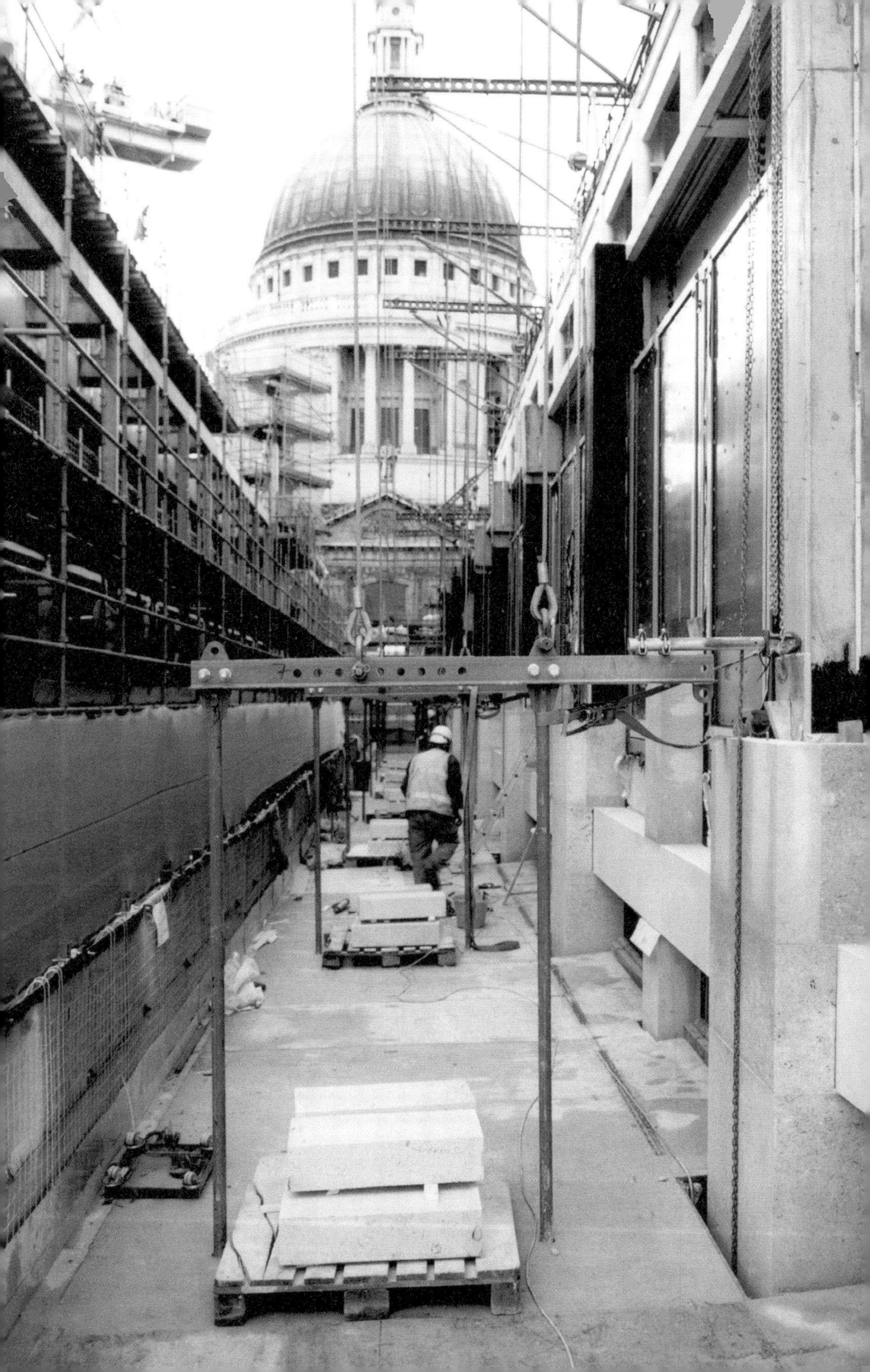

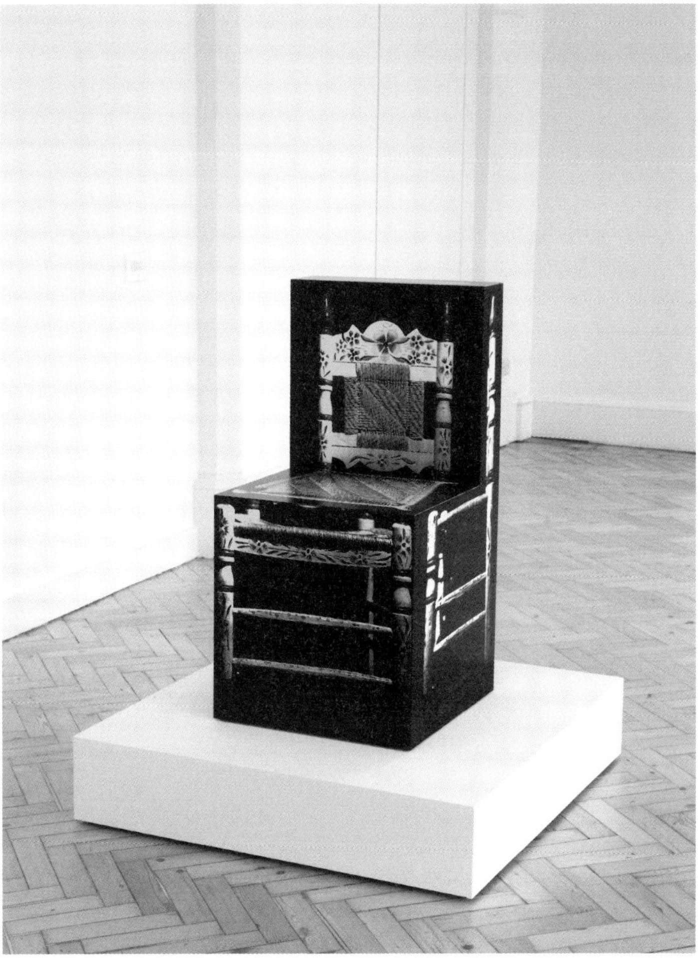

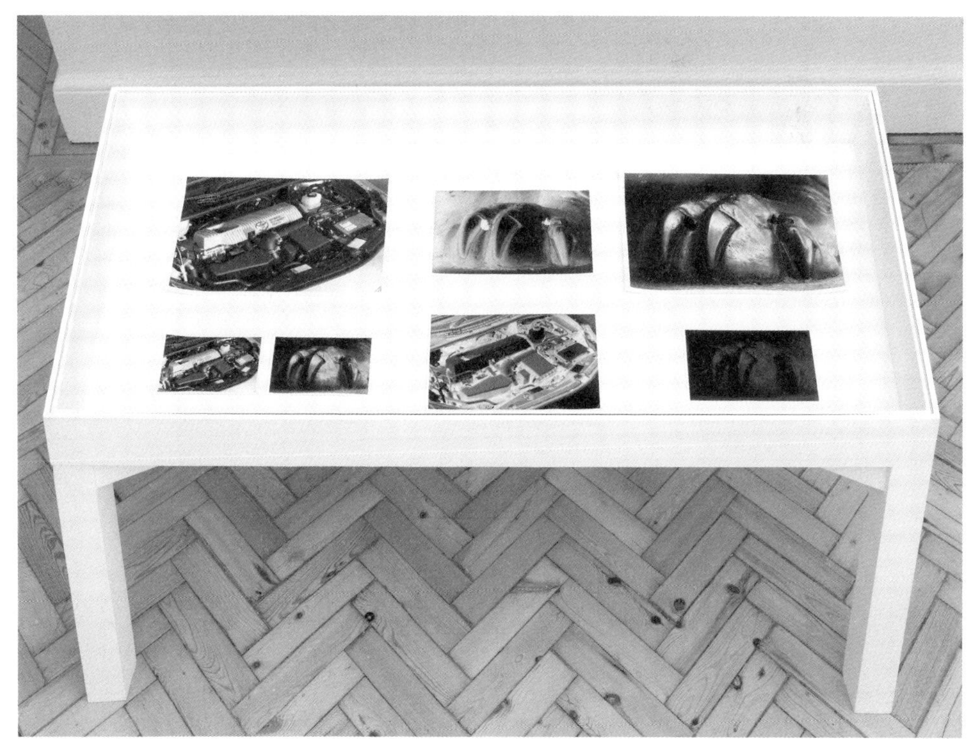

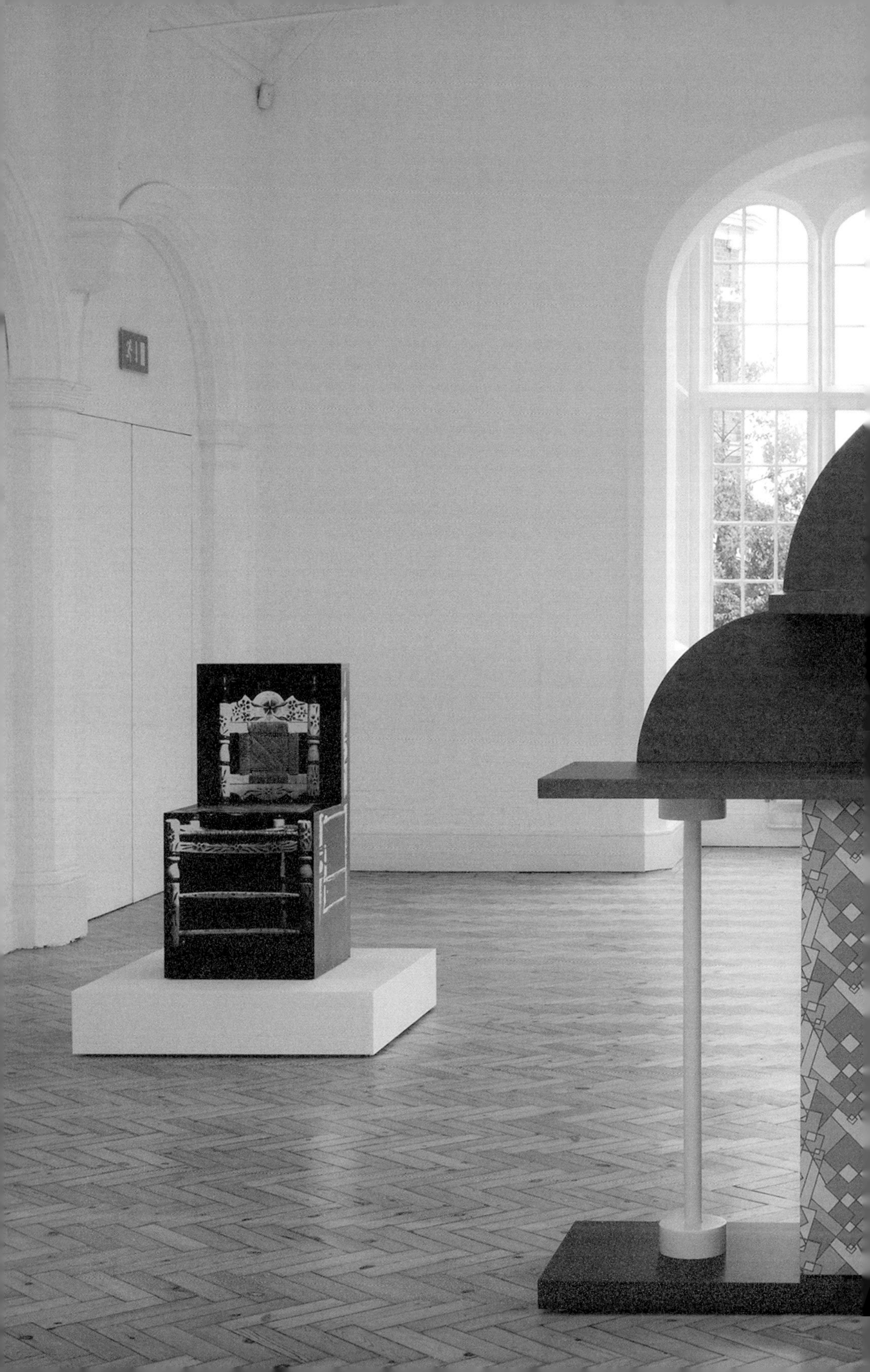

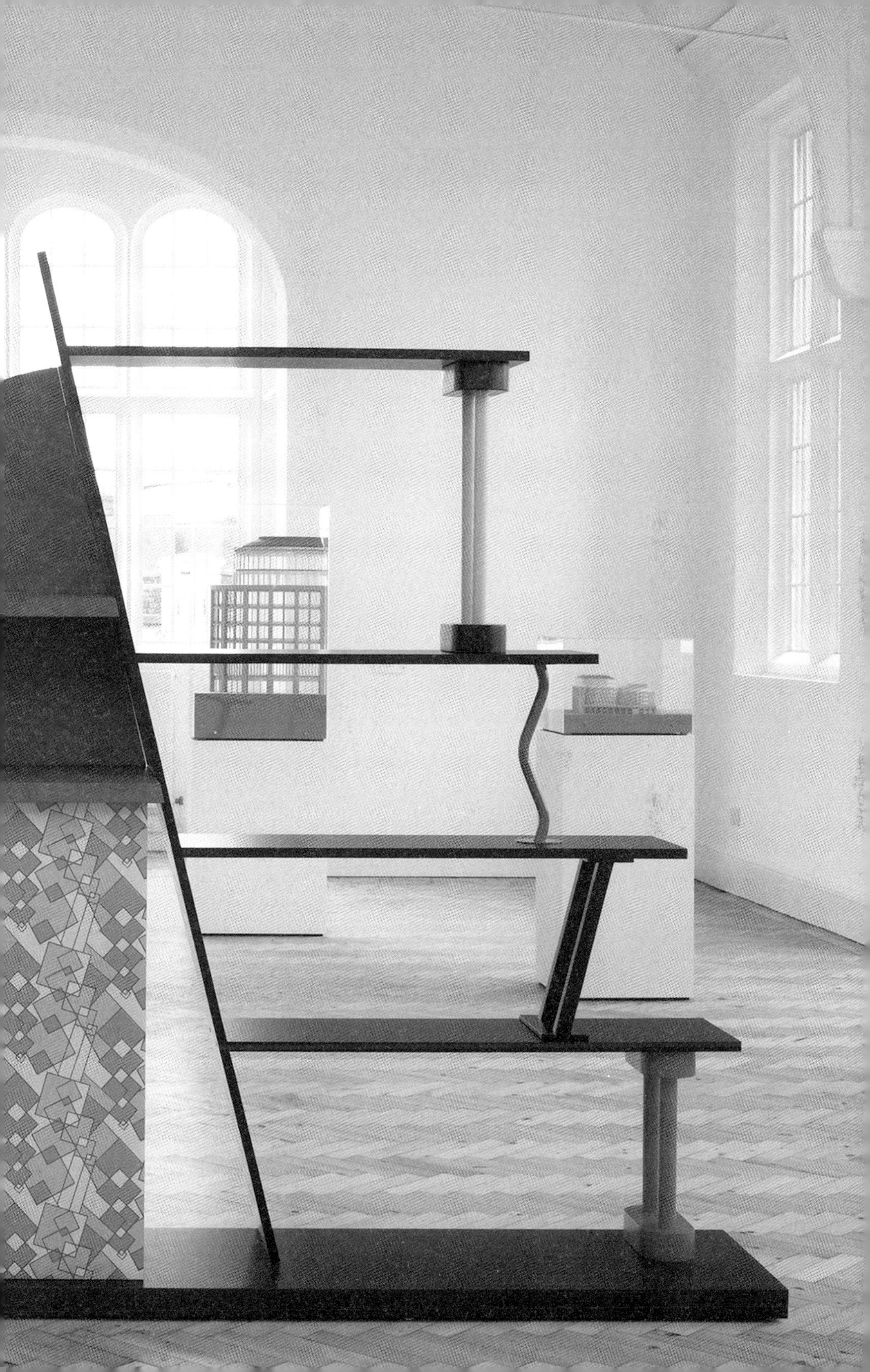

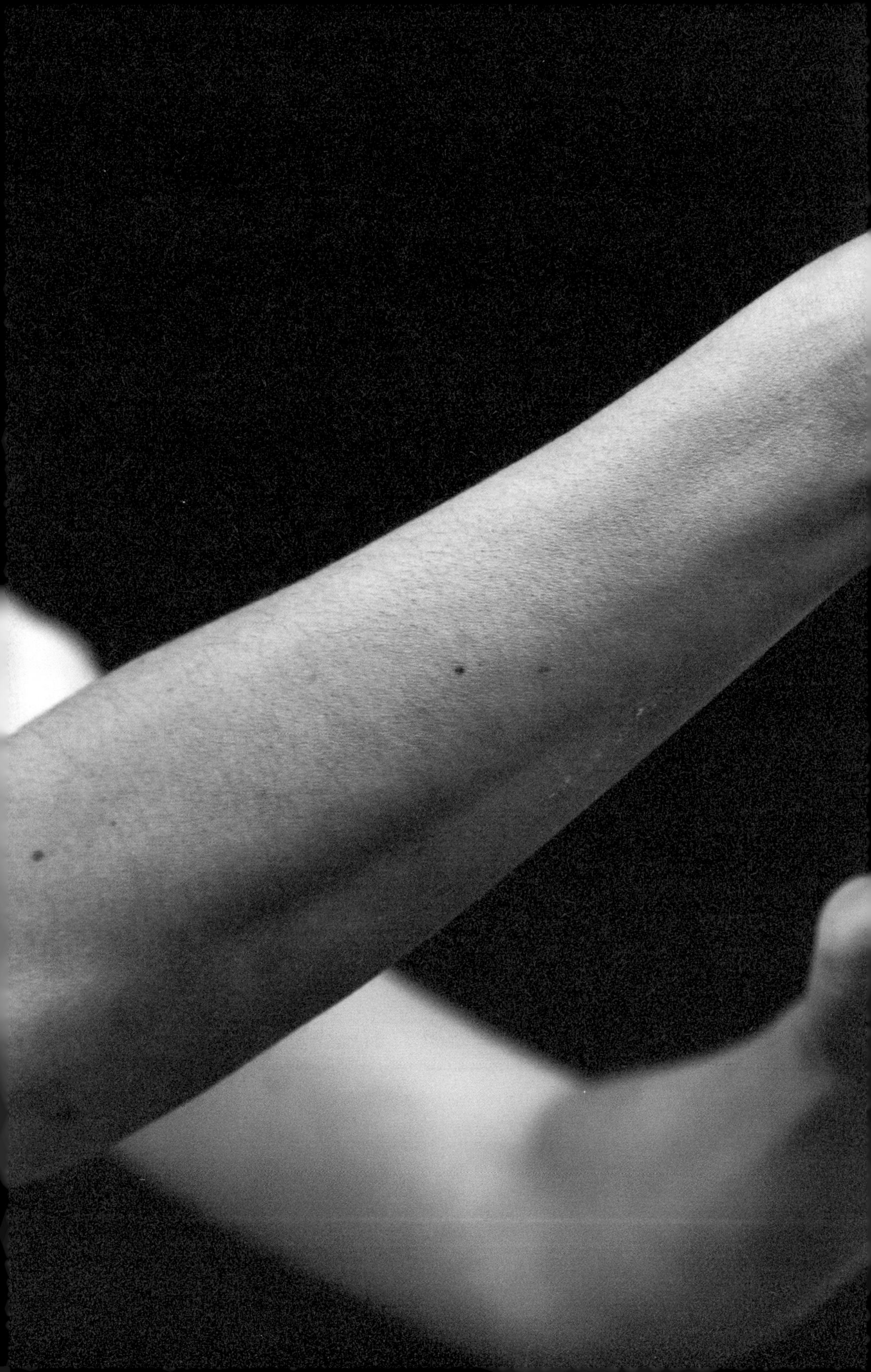

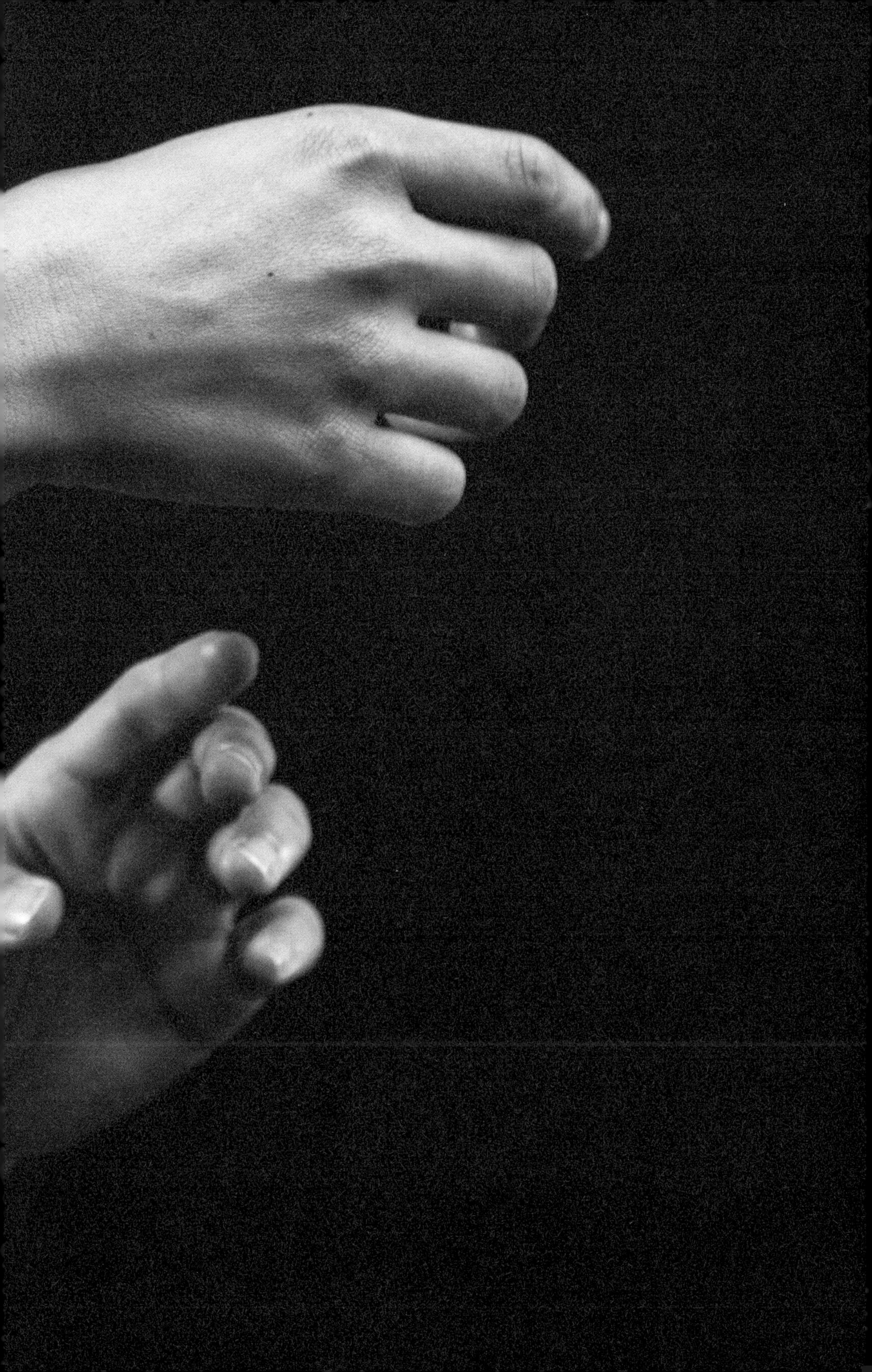

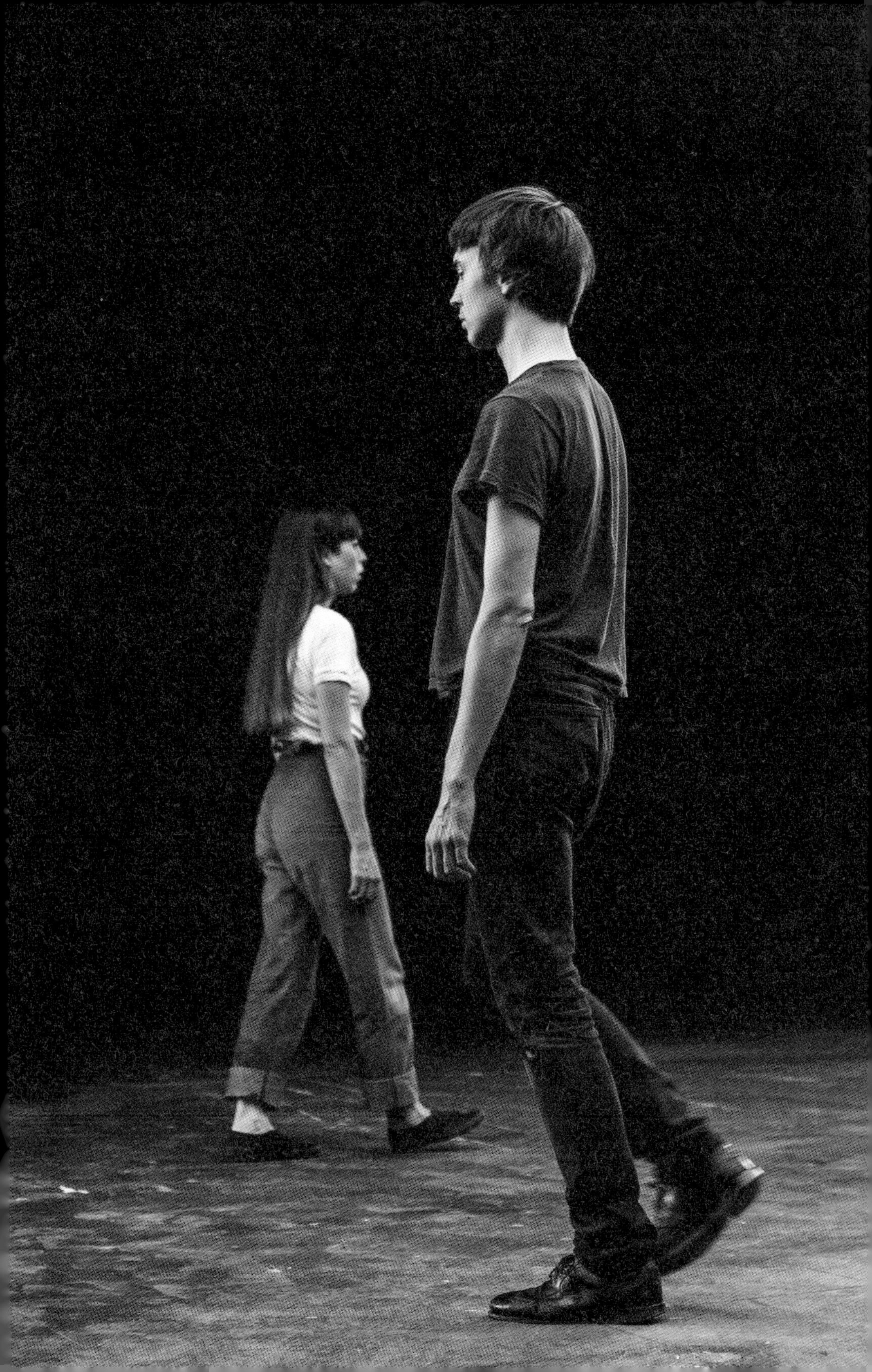

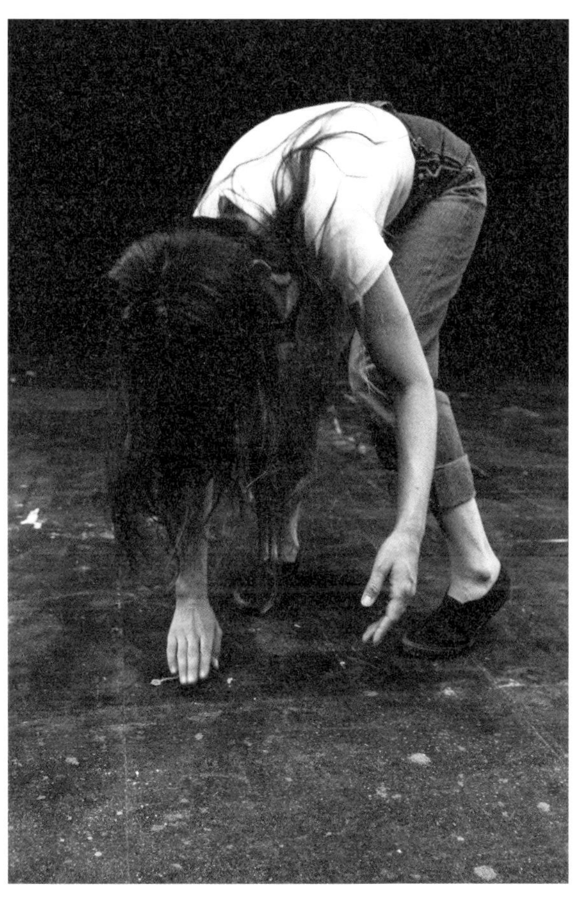

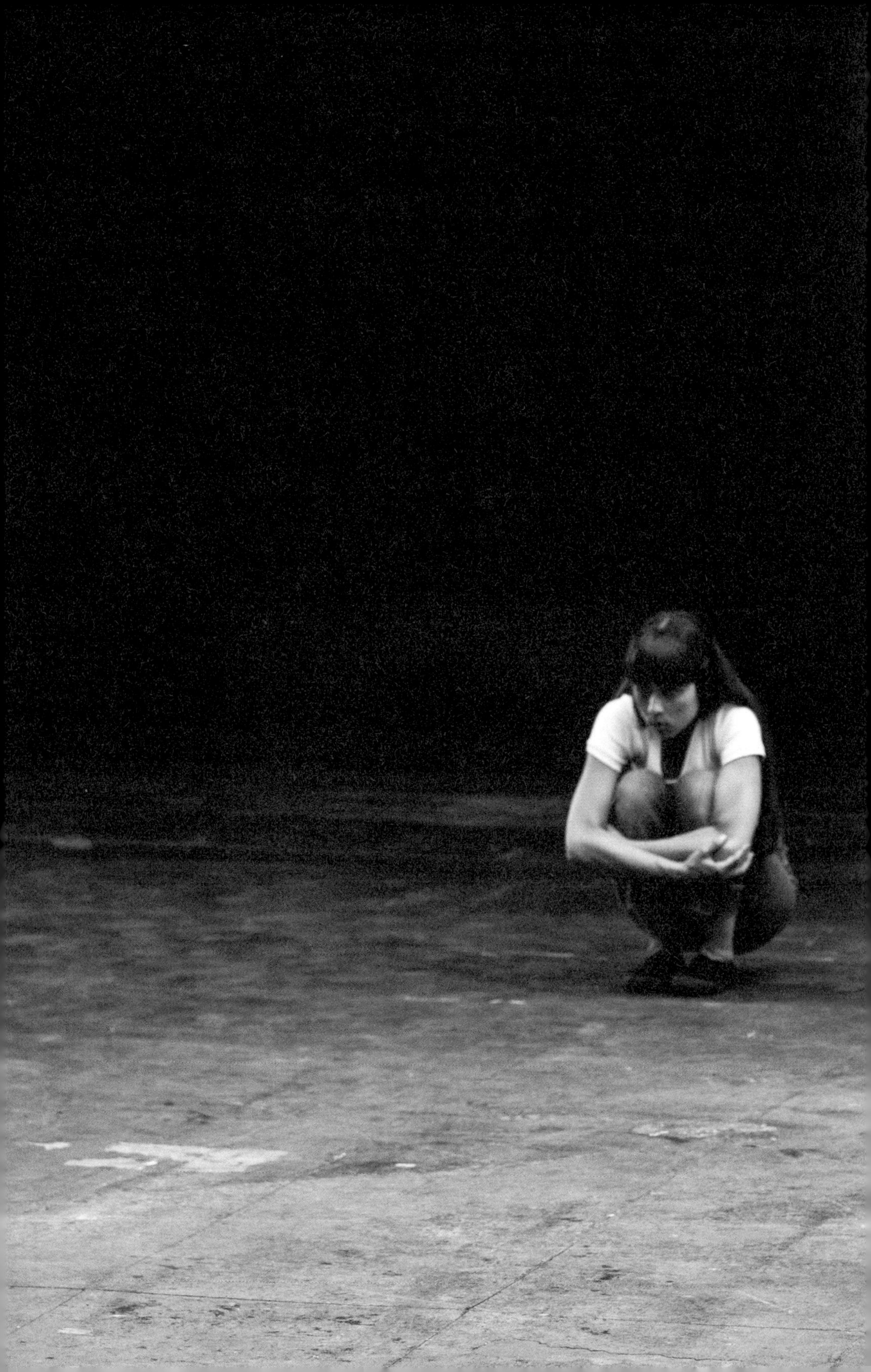

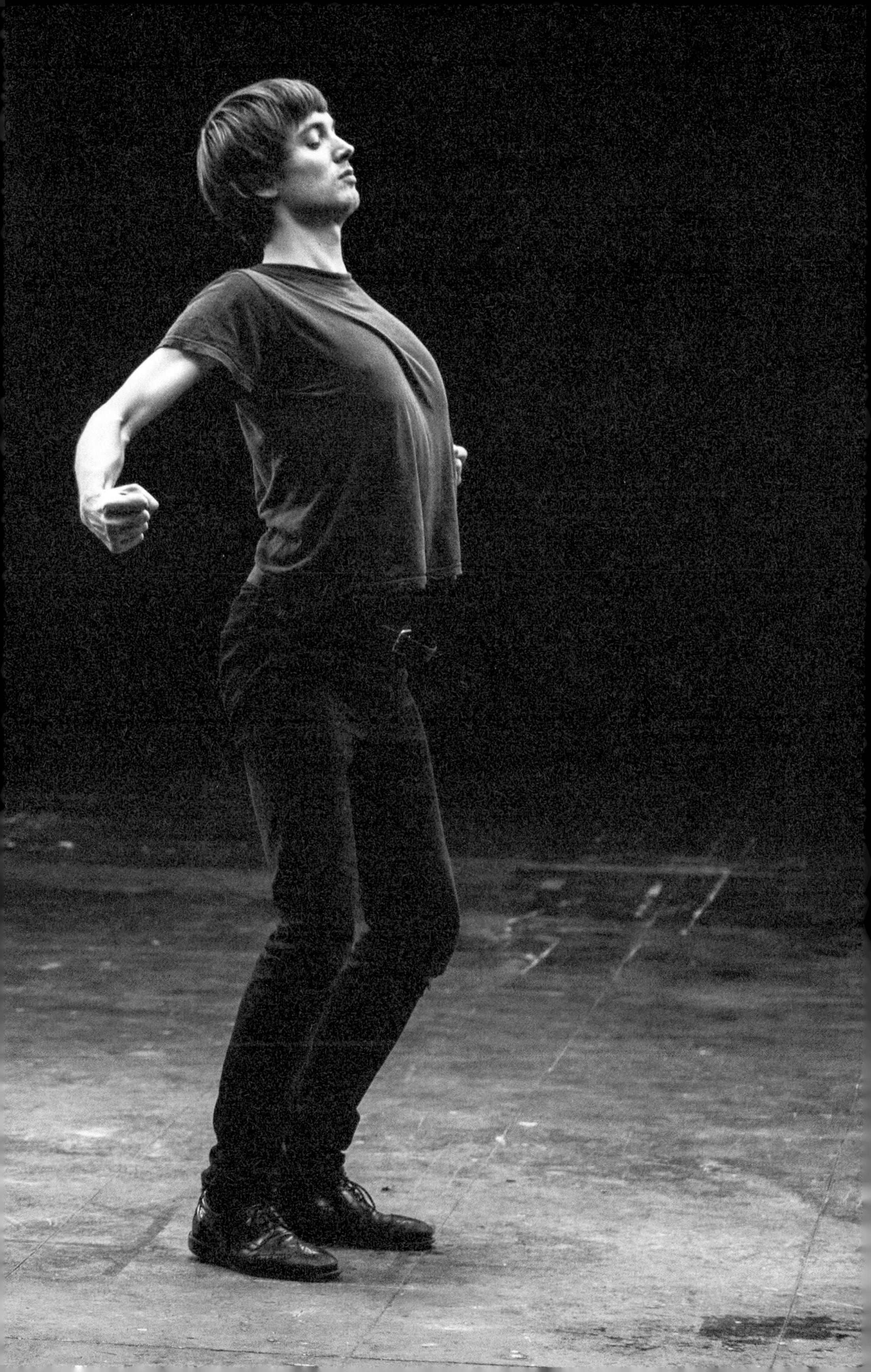

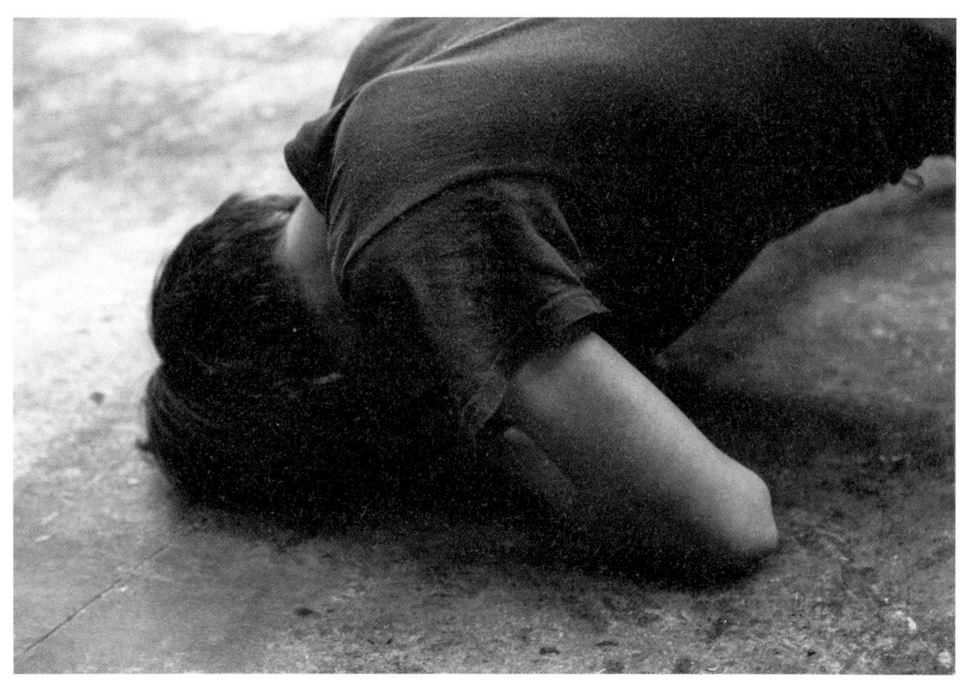

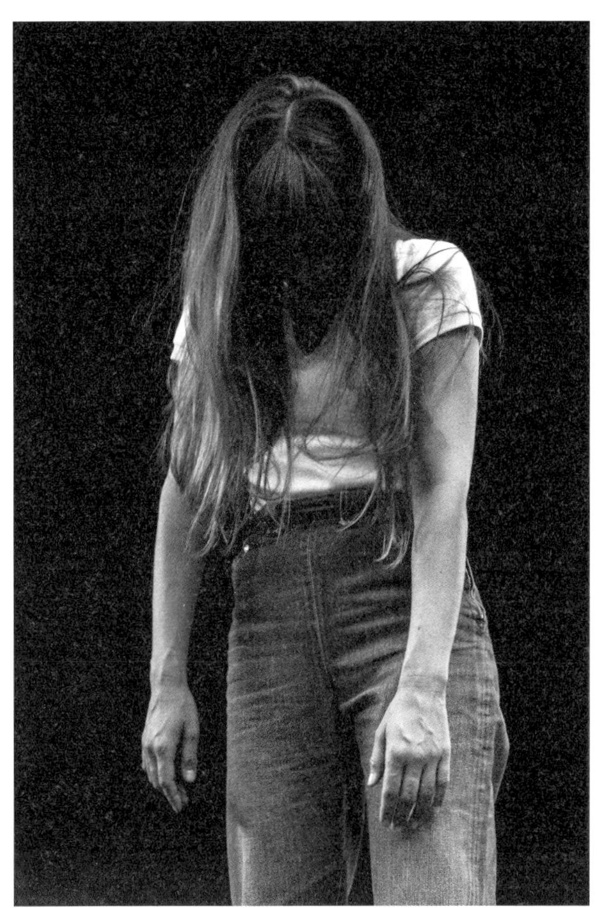

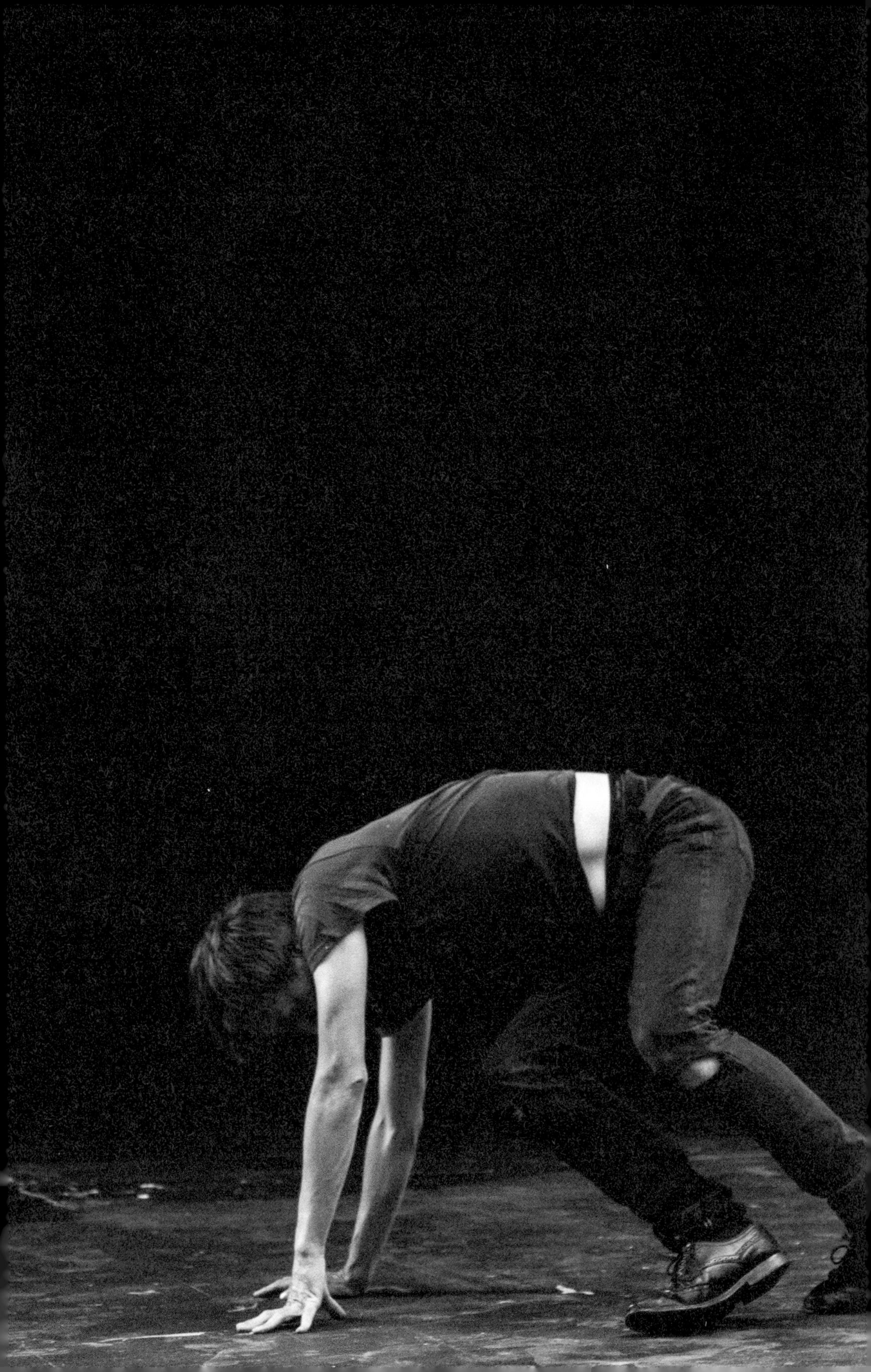

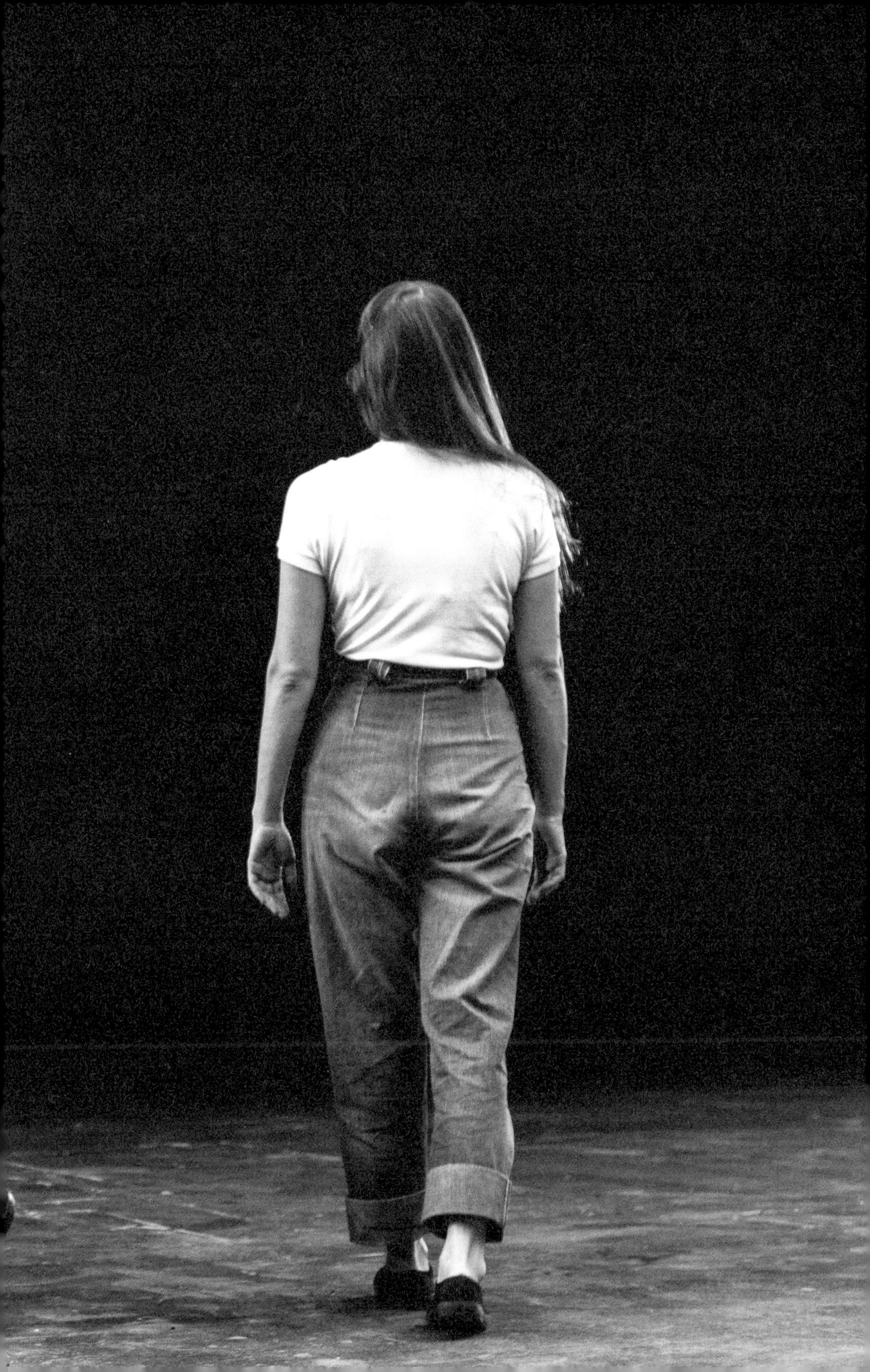

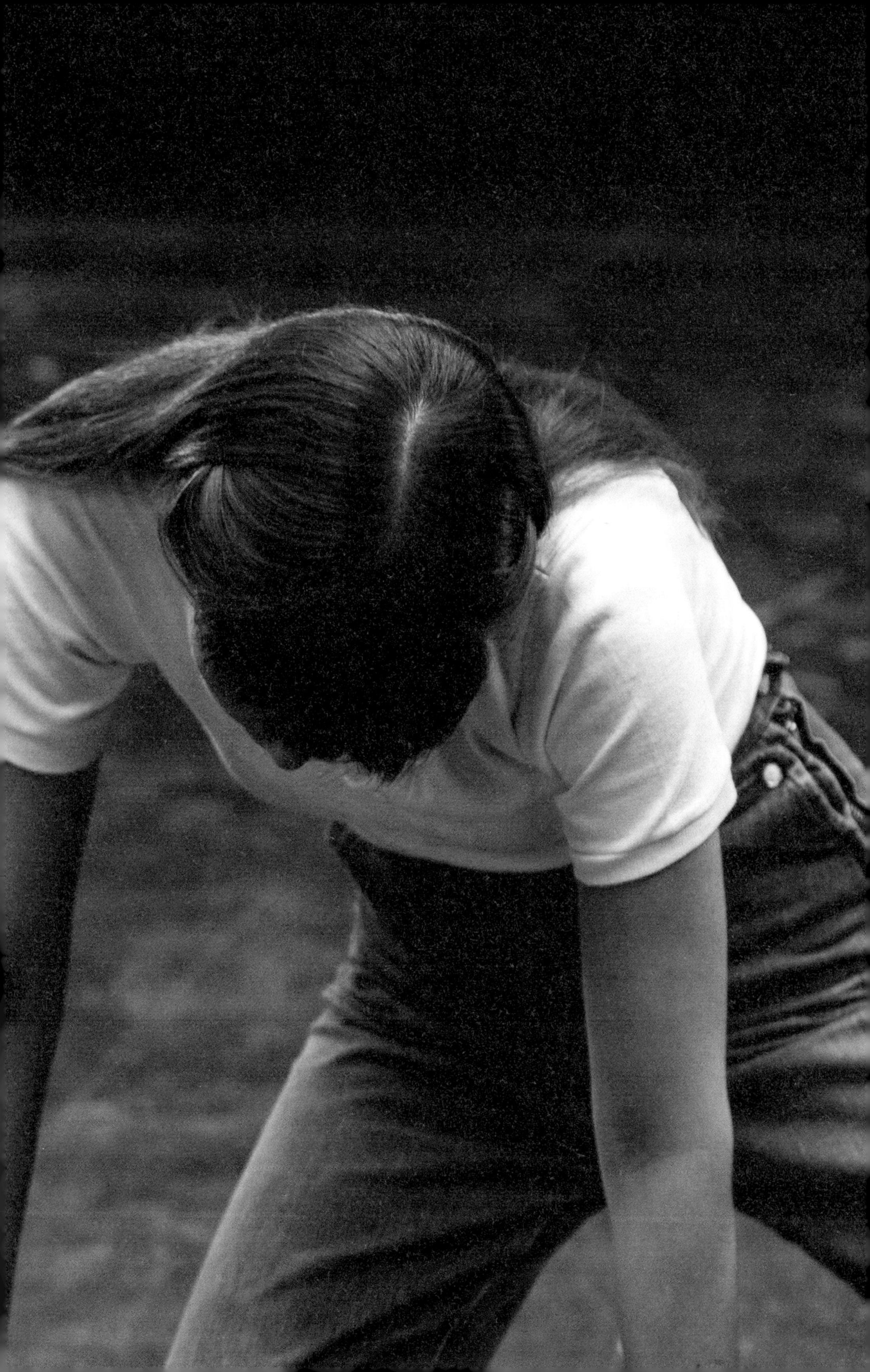

Simon Martin
Born in Cheshire England, 1965. Mid-Cheshire College of Art & Design,
1984–85. Slade School of Art, University College, London, 1985–89.
Lives and works in London.

Selected Solo Exhibitions
Camden Arts Centre, London (2015); Focal Point Gallery, Southend-
on-Sea (offsite commission 2014); Northern Gallery for Contemporary
Art, Sunderland (2013); Camden Arts Centre, London (2012); Holburne
Museum, Bath (2012); Collective Gallery, Edinburgh (2012); Kunstverein
Amsterdam, Amsterdam (2010); HIT, Gothenburg (2010); Bass Museum
of Art, Miami (2008); Chisenhale Gallery, London (2008); Lightbox Tate
Britain, London (2008); Carl Freedman Gallery, London (2006); The Power
Plant Contemporary Art Gallery, Toronto (2006); White Columns, New York
(2005); Counter Gallery, London (2005); Counter Gallery, London (2003);
Poster Project, Dublin (2003); Mellow Birds, London (2001); Javier Lopez
Gallery, London (1995); Glasshouse, London (1994).

Selected Group Exhibitions
The Parliament of Things, Firstsite, Colchester (2015); *The Event Sculpture*,
Henry Moore Institute, Leeds (2014); *Glasgow International*, Kelvingrove
Museum, Glasgow (2014); *The Imaginary Museum*, Kunstverein, Munich
(with Ed Atkins) (2012); *How to Look at Everything*, The Common Guild,
Glasgow (2012); *British Art Show 7: In the Days of the Comet*, Nottingham
Contemporary, Nottingham; CCA, Glasgow; Tramway, Glasgow and
Plymouth Arts Consortium (2011); *Taipei Biennial*, Taipei, Taiwan (2010);
Strange Events Permit Themselves The Luxury Of Occurring, Camden
Arts Centre, London (2007); *Cocaine Orgasm*, BANK, London (1995).

Martin was the recipient of a Paul Hamlyn Award (2008) and shortlisted
for the Jarman Award (2009).

List of works

Carlton

pp.52–9
Simon Martin
Carlton, 2006
Film stills
Courtesy Simon Martin

pp.62–3
Installation view, The Common Guild,
Glasgow, 2012

Louis Ghost Chair

pp.44–7
Simon Martin
Louis Ghost Chair, 2012
Production stills
Courtesy FVU
Photography: David Pearson
Thanks to the Frederick Parker Custodians of
the Worshipful Company of Furniture Makers

pp.67–8
Simon Martin
Louis Ghost Chair, 2012
Installation view, Northern Gallery
for Contemporary Art Sunderland

pp.70–5
Simon Martin displayed a series of photographs
of traditional African headrests as part of the
exhibition 'Louis Ghost Chair' at Collective,
Edinburgh, in 2012. The headrests are currently
held in the collection of National Museums
Scotland (NMS).
With thanks to Dr Sarah Worden, Senior Curator
of African Collections, NMS.

p.70
19th century wood and brass headrest from
Katanga, Democratic Republic of the Congo,
Central Africa

p.70
Early 20th century hardwood headrest from
Zimbabwe, Southern Africa

p.71
19th century hardwood headrest from
Mashonaland, Zimbabwe, southern Africa

p.71
19th century camwood headrest from the
Democratic Republic of the Congo, Central Africa

p.72
19th century wood and glass-bead headrest
from the Democratic Republic of the Congo,
Central Africa

p.72
19th century camwood headrest from the
Democratic Republic of the Congo, Central Africa

p.73
19th century hardwood headrest from Jubaland,
Somalia, East Africa

p.73
19th century wood headrest from Katanga,
Democratic Republic of the Congo, Central Africa

p.74
Late 19th / early 20th century hardwood headrest
from Malawi, Central Southern Africa

p.74
Early 20th century wood and pigment headrest
from Urua, Democratic Republic of the Congo,
Central Africa

p.75
Late 19th / early 20th century hardwood headrest
from South Africa / Mozambique

p.75
Late 19th century hardwood headrest from
Tanzania, East Africa

pp.78–9
Simon Martin
Untitled (After Donald Judd), 2011
Cadmium red light oil on wood with iron pipe
56 × 115 × 78 cm
'Priority Moments', Herald Street, London, 2011

pp.80–1
Simon Martin
Louis Ghost Chair, 2012
Production stills
Photography: David Pearson

UR Feeling

p.84
10 Paternoster Square, 2003
Courtesy Cristobal Palma

pp.86–9
In 2012, Camden Arts Centre, London, held an
exhibition by Simon Martin called 'UR Feeling',
featuring the artist's selection of artworks,
objects, talks and presentations that acted as
a preview and speculative research platform
for the video. The exhibition featured work by:
Richard Artschwager, Ettore Sottsass, Eric Parry
Architects, Stephen Shore, Malcolm Le Grice,
Emily Wardill, Dan Fox, Martino Gamper, Ben
Campkin, Rebecca Ross, Anna Minton and
Isobel Harbison.

pp.86, 88–9
Richard Artschwager
Chair 1965–2000, 1965–2000
Acrylic, paper and wood (edition 3/6)
103 × 52 × 51 cm
Private Collection, Germany
Courtesy Sprüth Magers, Berlin & London

p.87
Simon Martin
Untitled, 2012
Seven photographic prints

pp.88–9
Ettore Sottsass
Malabar, room divider, 1982
Wood, plastic laminate, enameled metal
230 × 254 × 60.5 cm
Courtesy MEMPHIS-MILANO,
Pregnana Milanese

pp.88–9
Eric Parry Architects
*Architectural models for
10 Paternoster Square*
152 × 93 × 88 cm
36 × 46 × 51 cm
Courtesy Eric Parry Architects

pp.90–100
Simon Martin
UR Feeling, 2015
Production stills
Photography: Mark Blower

Film credits

Carlton, 2006
Produced, directed and edited by Simon Martin
Director of Photography: Mattias Nyberg
Voiceover artist: Abigail Hayes

Louis Ghost Chair, 2012
Commissioned by Film and Video Umbrella (FVU)
and the Holburne Museum, Bath, in association
with Collective, Edinburgh, Northern Gallery
for Contemporary Art, Sunderland and Elena Hill.
Supported by Arts Council England with additional
support from Henry Moore Foundation.
Directed and edited by Simon Martin
Director of Photography: Martin Testar
Voiceover artist: Abigail Hayes
Producer: Cecilie Gravesen at FVU

UR Feeling, 2015
Commissioned by FLAMIN Productions through
Film London Artists' Moving Image Network
with funding from Arts Council England
Directed and edited by Simon Martin
Performers: Nissa Nishikawa, Martin Tomlinson
Director of Photography: Martin Testar
Editor: Daniel Goddard
Typography: Wolfram Wiedner
Producer: Tracy Bass
Production executives: Maggie Ellis
and Rose Cupit
Production assistant: Ester Catala
Production advisor: Pinky Ghundale

Simon Martin

Published by Film and Video Umbrella (FVU)
and Elena Hill

Edited by Steven Bode and Elena Hill,
and with thanks to Patrick Langley
Designed by Fraser Muggeridge studio

Publication supported by Arts Council England

© 2015, Film and Video Umbrella (FVU),
Elena Hill, the artist and the authors

ISBN: 978-1-904270-37-9

Film and Video Umbrella (FVU)
8 Vine Yard
London SE1 1QL
+44 (0)20 7407 7755
info@fvu.co.uk
www.fvu.co.uk

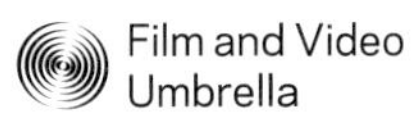

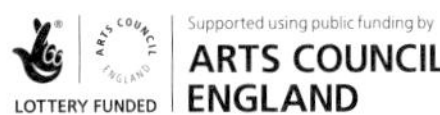

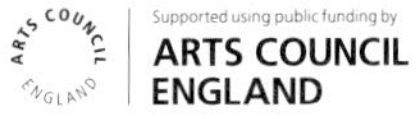

Simon Martin would like to thank:
Dan Fox, Melissa Gronlund and Neil Mulholland
(for their essays); Luke Hall at Fraser Muggeridge
studio (for his design); Tracy Bass; Martin Testar;
Jenni Lomax, Anne-Marie Watson, Gina Buenfeld
and the staff at Camden Arts Centre; Maggie
Ellis, Rose Cupit, Ester Catala, Pinky Ghundale
and Ian White at Film London. Special thanks to
Elena Hill and to Steven Bode, Cecilie Gravesen
and everyone at Film and Video Umbrella (FVU).

Film and Video Umbrella would like to thank:
Anna Mandlik at Arts Council England,
Kate Gray and Siobhan Carroll at Collective,
Edinburgh; Alistair Robinson at Northern
Gallery for Contemporary Art, Sunderland.
Special thanks to Nina Ernst.

Elena Hill would like to thank:
Ceri Johnston and Neil Harris at Arts Council
England, Dr. Alexander (Xa) Sturgis, Marnie
Whiting and Howard Batho at the Holburne
Museum, Anita Taylor and Pradeep Sharma,
Bath School of Art & Design, Kiera Hill.